DATE DUE

Library Management

LIBRARY SCIENCE TEXT SERIES

An Introduction to Classification and Number Building in Dewey. By Marty Bloomberg and Hans Weber.

Introduction to Public Services for Library Technicians. 2nd ed. By Marty Bloomberg.

Introduction to Technical Services for Library Technicians. 3rd ed. By Marty Bloomberg and G. Edward Evans.

A Guide to the Library of Congress Classification. By John Phillip Immroth.

Science and Engineering Literature: A Guide to Reference Sources. 2nd ed. By H. Robert Malinowsky, Richard A. Gray, and Dorothy A. Gray.

The Vertical File and Its Satellites: A Handbook of Acquisition, Processing and Organization. By Shirley Miller.

Introduction to United States Public Documents. By Joe Morehead.

The School Library Media Center. By Emanuel T. Prostano and Joyce S. Prostano.

The Humanities: A Selective Guide to Information Sources. By A. Robert Rogers.

The School Library and Educational Change. By Martin Rossoff.

Introduction to Library Science: Basic Elements of Library Service. By Jesse H. Shera.

The School Librarian as Educator. By Lillian Biermann Wehmeyer.

Introduction to Cataloging and Classification. 5th ed. By Bohdan S. Wynar, with the assistance of John Phillip Immroth.

Library Management

Robert D. Stueart
John Taylor Eastlick

Libraries Unlimited, Inc.
Littleton, Colo.

1977

LIBRARIES UNLIMITED, INC.
P.O. Box 263
Littleton, Colorado 80160

Library of Congress Cataloging in Publication Data

Stueart, Robert D
   Library management.

   (Library science text series)
   Includes bibliographical references and index.
   1. Library administration. I. Eastlick, John T.,
joint author. II. Title.
Z678.S799   658'.91'02   76-49568
ISBN 0-87287-127-4

TABLE OF CONTENTS

2—THE PLANNING PROCESS (cont'd)

LIST OF ILLUSTRATIONS

To Marlies and Virginia

PREFACE

The purpose of this book is to present the principles of management for libraries and information centers in a conceptual framework. Thus, this volume can serve the needs of both practitioners and students, both as a text for formal classroom situations and as a guide for self-instructed or group-related continuing education. The genesis of this volume comes from the almost total void that exists in the area of writings on library management. Some important articles have begun to appear in the last 10 years, and some texts have appeared concerning special types of libraries (school, media centers, community college, college, university, public and special), but there has been no comprehensive approach to the management of libraries. The intent of this volume, then, is to examine the dynamics of the library as an organization—the behavior of individuals and groups within the library, the policies and programs of the library, and the relationship of the library to its staff and its clientele.

The challenge of management in libraries has increased tremendously in recent years, influenced to a great degree by the rapid advance of technology and the expanding scope of library and information center activities, which has made many libraries into large, complex organizations.

Although most would agree that the principles of management are applicable to all types and sizes of enterprises, this volume presents those principles and theories in the context of libraries and information centers. It is assumed that techniques such as case studies, in-basket exercises, action mazes, and other simulated techniques will be used to supplement and magnify the principles that are important to management and that are developed here.

In preparing for the management "jungle," one should keep in mind that anyone who is supervising another—whether this is another professional, a paraprofessional, a clerical, or a student assistant—is involved in the management process. Analysis of the workings of organizations shows that management must use the theories and techniques of many disciplines. For example, planning cannot be done without forecasting, and this requires some knowledge of economics. Despite the documented advantages of combining theory with practice in operating an organization, many discount the importance of theory in a practical situation. There are practitioners who refuse to acknowledge that principles of management exist, but these same people must, in reality, apply the principles every day in their work situation. For instance, decisions, if they are rational, are always based on some theory, whether or not we are aware of the theoretical basis. Even a "hunch" has a theoretical base. The manager must also be concerned with the human aspect and must be familiar with the conceptual framework of managing.

We have used the "traditional" headings which relate to planning, organizing, staffing, directing, and controlling simply to categorize discussion. This volume is arranged according to those five basic principles. Other writers would perhaps break down the functions in a different way, but this arrangement combines some principles and makes for what the authors feel is a better organization of the text. Needless to say the actual operation of a library or information center follows no such precise linear pattern, for almost all elements are progressing simultaneously and they usually do not occur in a hierarchical relationship. Each idea, each concept discussed is related to or builds upon others.

In writing this volume the authors have drawn freely upon research and writings in the fields of business management, public administration, and related fields of the social sciences. The text also reflects the authors' experience, at all management levels, in both public and academic libraries. Their experience in teaching management to graduate students in universities and colleges and their participation—often as leaders—in workshops, institutes, and seminars on many aspects of management, have also been helpful in organizing the concepts and examples used in this volume. These experiences, readings, writings and teachings have blended together to form the basis for this volume.

The authors wish to acknowledge the encouragement and patience which has been given us by the publishers, Libraries Unlimited, and the willing help of Kathy Peroni, Norma Burchard, James Foyle, and Richard Lietz.

Robert D. Stueart
Simmons College
Boston, Massachusetts

John Taylor Eastlick
University of Denver
Denver, Colorado

1

MANAGEMENT DEVELOPMENT:
An Historical Overview

Management has been of some concern to organized society throughout civilized history, although its systematic study as a separate branch of human knowledge is fairly recent. The epoch of management inquiry and research has largely developed during this century, and many schools of thought have tried to formulate the underlying principles of management.

As early as 3000 B.C., the Sumerians kept records on clay tablets; many of those records applied to the management practices of the priests in Ur. The Babylonians also produced laws regulating business enterprise, through the Hammurabian code. Later, during Nebuchadnezzar's reign, they produced a number of managerial feats including the Hanging Gardens of Babylon.

Interpretations of early Egyptian papyri, extending as far back as 1300 B.C., indicate that the bureaucratic states of antiquity recognized the importance of organization and administration. Similar records exist for ancient China. Confucius' parables include practical suggestions for proper public administration.

Although the records of early Greece do not give much insight into the principles of management, the very existence of the Athenian commonwealth, with its councils, popular courts, administrative officials, and board of generals, indicates an appreciation of the managerial function. Socrates' definition of management as a skill separate from technical knowledge and experience is remarkably close to current understanding of the function.

It is known that in ancient Rome the complexity of the administrative job evoked considerable development of management techniques. It is thought that the Roman Empire's secret of success lay in the ability of the Romans to organize. Even Hannibal's crossing of the Alps in 218 B.C., with his Carthaginian troops and equipment, was a remarkable organizational feat.

Many of the techniques that we employ today in modern organizations can be traced to ancient origins. For instance, the first record of motion studies came from the time of Cyrus, the Persian King, in about 600 B.C. These records indicate that flute and pipe governed the motions, with songs for each task. They introduced rhythm, standard motion, and work tempo.

By age, the most efficient formal organization in the history of Western civilization has been the Catholic Church. This is due not only to the appeal of its objectives but also to the effectiveness of its organization and management techniques. The scalar chain of command was introduced early in the organization of the Church, as was the concept of specialization.

Machiavelli, in his writings of the early 1500s, emphasized the principle that authority developed from the consent of the masses. His ideas, particularly as set forth in *The Prince*, have application to our current study of leadership and communications.

Some of the most important principles and practices of modern business management can be traced to military organizations. Although such organizations were fairly simple until recent times, they have gradually improved their techniques of direction. Among the most important of these has been the staff principle. The "general staff," for example, organized under a chief of staff, furnished specialized advice and information and supplied auxiliary services that have come to be essential features of military and business enterprise. The line of command concept also had its origin in the armies of antiquity and medieval ages, and the scalar principle is still a very important part of military organizations today.

The development of technology during the Industrial Revolution produced a factory system that brought workers into a central location and into contact with other workers. It was during the development of effective and efficient management control of those newly founded organizations that many management concepts began to emerge. Adam Smith in his writings, and particularly in *The Wealth of Nations*, described the "division of work" as it should be employed in organizations. Other writers of that period, including Robert Owen, Charles Babbage and Charles Dupin, wrote on the problems of management in factories.[1] Many of the principles that were later reemphasized and further refined in both the scientific management school and the human relations school were actually first developed by those writers during the eighteenth and nineteenth centuries. For instance, Babbage in his writing encouraged managers to use time study techniques, centralize production, inaugurate research and development, etc.[2]

Various methods have been used in the study of administration in this century. The first systematic approach was legalistic, being devoted to a study of the organization, powers, and activities and limitations of the public authorities. Later, a more scientific approach was used, concerned chiefly with administrative organization as the instrument of management. An attempt was made to determine, on the basis of empirical evidence, rules for efficient and effective administrative organization and operation. More recently the behaviorists have been using the methods of psychology, sociology, and anthropology in an effort to secure a better understanding of group behavior, leadership, and decision-making. This is now a major movement. These "schools" are referred to differently in different texts, but the content of each school is more or less defined so that it can be recognized.

No student can afford not to be familiar with the ideas of some pioneer thinkers in the field. This is not to say that their ideas should be accepted without question. However, the ideas of those thinkers are the basis for the development of management as we know it today, and these "schools" provide insight into the essence of management. As Harold Koontz puts it:

> There are the behaviorists . . . who see management as a complex of interpersonal relationships and the basis of management theory the tentative tenets of the new and undeveloped science of psychology. There are also those who see management theory as simply a manifestation of the institutional and cultural aspects of sociology. Still

others, observing that the central core of management is decision-making, branch in all directions from this core to encompass everything in organization life. Then, there are mathematicians, who think of management primarily as an exercise in logical relationships expressed in symbols and the omnipresent and ever revered model. But the entanglement of growth reaches its ultimate when the study of management is regarded as one of a number of systems and subsystems, with an understandable tendency for the researcher to be dissatisfied until he has encompassed the entire physical and cultural universe as a management system.[3]

It is apparent, from studying the schools of management thought which have developed in this century, that they reflect the problems of the times in which they were popular. A few of them have survived and are influencing management thought today. For purposes of discussion, these can be grouped into the Scientific, Human Relations, and Decision Theory Schools.

SCIENTIFIC SCHOOLS

Scientific Management School

The basic assumption of this school is the philosophy that workers are economically motivated and that they will respond with their best efforts if material rewards are closely related to work efforts. The emphasis is on maximum output with minimum effort by eliminating waste and inefficiency at the operative level. In the United States, the work of Frederick Winslow Taylor dominates the thinking in this field of management. Taylor expounded several basic principles:

1) To gather all traditional knowledge and classify, tabulate, and reduce it to rules, laws, and formulas so as to help workers in their daily work.
2) To develop a science for each element of man's work to replace the rule-of-thumb method.
3) To scientifically select and then train, teach, and develop the worker.
4) To cooperate with workers to ensure that work is done according to developed scientific principles.
5) To effect an almost equal division of work and responsibility between workers and managers; that is, managers are to be given work for which they are best fitted, as are employees.[4]

Efficiency was the central theme of Taylor's writings. A steel works manager in Philadelphia, he was interested in knowing how to get more work out of workers, who are "naturally lazy and engage in systematic soldiering." This attitude was contributed to by poor management. He observed "when a naturally energetic man works for a few days beside a lazy one, the logic of the situation is unanswerable. 'Why should I work hard when the lazy fellow gets the same pay that I do and does only half as much work?' "[5] He proposed using scientific research methods to discover the best way. He felt that faster work could be assured only through 1) enforced standardization of methods; 2) enforced adaptation of best instruments and working conditions; and 3) enforced cooperation. He performed several experiments:

1) **Work Study.** One experiment detailed movements of workers in a shop and suggested short cuts or more efficient ways of performing certain operations. Within three years the output of the shop had doubled.

2) **Standardized tools for shops.** In another area he found that the coal shovels being used weighed from 16 to 38 pounds. After experimenting, it was found that 21-22 pounds was the best weight. Again after three years 140 men were doing what had previously been done by between 400 and 600 men.

3) **Selection and training of workers.** Taylor insisted that each worker be assigned to do what he was best suited for and that those who exceeded the defined work be paid "bonuses." Production, as might be expected, rose to an all-time high.

Taylor, therefore, advocated assignment of supervisors by "function"–i.e., one for training, one for discipline, etc. This functional approach is evident today in many organizations, including libraries.

Needless to say, his efforts were resented by workers and managers alike. He was fired from his original job in Philadelphia. He then went to Bethlehem Steel, where he was again fired after three years. The unions, indignant by this time, obtained investigation of his methods by a special congressional committee and were successful in forbidding "stop watches" or "bonuses" in Army arsenals until World War II. However, Eastern shipping concerns adopted his techniques and their popularity grew. The concepts spread to Europe and Britain and received impetus in Russia after the Revolution. Many maintain that this school represents techniques only and "hinders" a philosophy.

Taylor was the most important advocate of the scientific method approach, but there were others who worked in the same area. Frank and Lillian Gilbreth, authors of *Cheaper by the Dozen*, were contemporaries of Taylor. Frank, an engineer, and Lillian, a Ph.D. in psychology, expanded the concepts of motion study and fatigue. They devised the "one best way," which involved the fewest motions performed in the most comfortable position. They identified 17 basic elements in on-the-job motions (such as "grasp," "hold," "position," "search," etc.). These motions were called THERBLIGS, Gilbreth spelled backward, with one transposition.[6]

Taylor's work and the Gilbreths' work were complementary–Taylor stressed time study and the Gilbreths, motion study. Out of these two systems emerged the industrial engineering discipline.

Henry L. Gantt, of the Gantt Chart fame, writing and experimenting at the same time, developed the task-and-bonus system which was similar to Taylor's awards incentive. Along the horizontal axis, the Gantt Chart shows time, work schedule, and work completed, and along the vertical axis it shows the individuals and machines assigned to those schedules.

Classical School

Another "school," which began to develop in France at about the same time as Taylor's experiment in the United States, purports to analyze the management process, establish a conceptual framework for it, identify principles, and build a theory of management from them. It regards management as a universal process. This school, most often called the classical school, is sometimes referred to as the "traditional" or "universalist" school. Just as Taylor is considered the father of the Scientific Management School, the father of the classical school is a Frenchman, Henri Fayol. In his works, Fayol took the scientific approach, but he looked at administration from the top down. He emphasized the need to teach administration schools at all levels. Briefly, his stated principles were:

1) **Division of work.** As the enterprise grows, there should be an early division of duties, and the activities concerning management should be separated out and become distinct. Specialization naturally develops with division of work.

2) **Authority.** The authority that individuals possess in an organization should be equal to their given responsibility. If one is responsible for the results of a task, that person should be given the authority to take actions necessary to ensure its success.

3) **Discipline.** There should be complete obedience, energy, and behavior in the best interest of the organization.

4) **Unity of command.** An employee should receive orders from only one superior. (This unity of command was in direct opposition to Taylor's idea of having workers take instructions from several "foremen.")

5) **Unity of direction.** A body with two heads is a monster and has difficulty in surviving. There should be one head and one plan to ensure a coordinated effort.

6) **Subordination of individual interest to general interest.** Primary concern should be the growth of the organization.

7) **Remuneration of personnel.** Wages should be fair.

8) **Centralization.** Everything that goes to increase the importance of the subordinate's role is decentralization, everything that goes to reduce it is centralization. Centralization is the desirable arrangement within an organization.

9) **Scalar chain.** Gangplanks should be used to prevent the scalar chain from bogging down. The gangplank (dotted line in Figure 1-1) can be thrown across without weakening the chain of command, as long as this relationship is advisory and not policy making.

Figure 1-1
Gangplank Principle

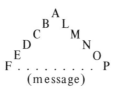

(message)

10) **Order.** There is a right place for everything and everyone in the organization. That place or job must be identified.

11) **Equity.** Equality of treatment must be taken into account in dealing with employees. Justice should be tempered with kindness.

12) **Stability of tenure of personnel.** It is important to keep people on the job.

13) **Initiative.** Incentive rewards may be provided to stimulate production.

14) **Esprit de corps.** Communication is the key to a satisfied working group.[7]

Fayol considered qualities required by managers as physical (health, vigor); mental (ability to understand and learn, judgment, and adaptability); moral (energy, firmness, willingness to accept responsibility, initiative, loyalty, tact, dignity); educational (general acquaintance with matters not belonging exclusively to the function performed); technical (peculiar to the function); and related to experience (arising from the work proper).

Fayol saw workers as people who: 1) are naturally lazy; 2) resist work more effectively when working in groups; 3) must be subjected to sharp discipline; 4) can best be motivated by the incentive of higher wages; 5) can do much better when properly instructed; and 6) differ markedly in native ability and capacity. However, he was more concerned than Taylor was with human relations. He was more concerned with defining the activities of managers and thus the division of labor. He and Luther Gulick, among others, advised managers to break down complicated jobs into more specialized activities. This was achieved through a "pyramid of control."

Taylor and Fayol, then, may be considered the founders of the theory of administration or management. There is little doubt that many organizations, including libraries, still depend heavily on these classical theories for the bases of their formal organizations. The greatest criticisms of these schools have been that they placed undue emphasis on the formal aspects of organization and neglected entirely the effects of individual personality, informal groups, intra-organizational conflicts, and decision-making process on the formal structure.

System School

World War I gave great impetus to the study of efficiency and by 1930 the idea of applying theory to organization and system was emphasized in the organization and system school. This theory distinguished between administration (representing the ownership point of view) and scientific management (that is, approach to work at the operative level) as they related to organization and system. This school expanded the work of Fayol and at the same time began to explore the behavioral aspects of management. For example, Max Weber and his disciples, studying bureaucracy, considered administrators as the key to governmental control in any modern state. As a structuralist, Weber, a German sociologist, emphasized specialization within an organization and gave a great deal of importance to the hierarchy of the decision-making process. Weber, writing about the same time as

Taylor and Fayol, analyzed the authority and responsibility of the "office" rather than the individual. The theory that he developed about authority structures in a complex organization is monumental.[8]

Other significant writers of this movement were Lyndell Urwick, an Englishman, and Luther Gulick, an American, who edited a landmark work on scientific administration.[9] Gulick, in a paper to President Roosevelt, in 1937, summed up an executive's functions in the acronym POSDCORB:

1) **P**lanning. That is, working out in broad outline the things that need to be done and the methods for doing them in order to accomplish the enterprise's set purpose.

2) **O**rganizing. That is, the establishment of the formal structure of authority through which work subdivisions are arranged, defined, and coordinated for the defined objectives.

3) **S**taffing. That is, the whole personnel function of bringing in and training the staff and maintaining favorable conditions for work.

4) **D**irecting. That is, the continuous task of making decisions and embodying them in specific and general orders and instructions and serving as the leader of the enterprise.

5) **CO**ordinating. That is, the all-important duty of interrelating the various parts of the work.

6) **R**eporting. That is, keeping those to whom the executive is responsible informed through records, research, and inspection.

7) **B**udgeting. This encompasses all that goes with budgeting in the form of fiscal planning, accounting, and control.

HUMAN RELATIONS SCHOOLS

Developing during the 1930s, the human relations schools compensated for some of the deficiencies of the classical theories. The thesis of the human relations schools is that, since managing involves getting things done through people, management study should center on interpersonal relations. The main emphasis of those schools, then, is on the individual and the informal group in the formal organization; it is concerned with integrating people into a work environment. The phrase "personnel administration" comes into prominence at this time, and increasing efforts toward democratization and staff participation are evident.

This "school" is primarily concerned with the study of people as human beings rather than as work units. A primary concern is the recognition of basic human needs, with the idea that once those needs are recognized and a willing ear is given to the suggestions and complaints, then morale will increase, as will production. Sociologists and psychologists have contributed to the development of this school.

Human Behavior School

Mary Follett, a political philosopher, emphasized the human aspect and called for intensive research within the organization. She was mainly concerned with the workers in the organization and their involvement in deciding their destiny within the organization. Early efforts into this type of research were the experiments of Elton Mayo and a group of industrial psychologists at the Western Electric Hawthorne Plant, in Chicago. These researchers began to study physical working conditions and their influence on worker productivity. Their studies revealed the importance of social interaction and psychological factors in determining productivity and satisfaction. Since that time, of course, behavioral scientists have refined the research tools used to evaluate human responses to their work environment. Several principles were demonstrated in their studies: 1) that workers are more motivated by social rewards and sanctions than by economic incentives; 2) that workers in their acts are influenced by the group; and 3) that whenever formal organizations exist, both formal and informal norms exist. They found that when the work group associated itself with management, productivity rose. When the group felt itself to be in opposition to management, productivity stayed close to the minimum accepted level. In general, the human behavior school maintains that if the organization makes employees happy, it will gain their full cooperation and effort, plus reaching optimum efficiency. Two other disciplines of this school are Rensis Likert and Frederick Herzberg.

It can be seen that Mayo's conclusions were quite different from those of Taylor. Taylor said that man at work is an entirely economic man; Mayo maintained that workers are motivated by "togetherness" and crave individual recognition within the group.

Social System School

This school is closely related to the human relations school and is often confused or intertwined with it. It encourages management to let employees develop social groups on the job, to move toward employee participation in management, and to allow democracy in the organization. The spiritual father of this school is perhaps Chester Barnard, who in his writings dwells on the contribution-satisfaction equilibrium and identifies four specific inducements: 1) material inducements (such as money and other physical securities); 2) personal non-material opportunities for distinction, prestige, and personal power; 3) desirable physical conditions of work; and 4) ideal benefactions, such as pride of workmanship, sense of adequacy, loyalty to the organization, etc.[10] Barnard emphasized communications as the "first function" of managers. Some prominent disciples of this school are Herbert Simon, Chris Argyris, Ralph Stogdill, Peter Drucker, Douglas McGregor, and Abraham Maslow.

Several new theories and concepts regarding the individual have emerged from the works of these authors. For instance, "Management by Objectives," a concept introduced in the 1950s by Peter Drucker, has been supported by Douglas McGregor in his "Theory Y." The idea is that information sharing is desirable and that management and workers should share planning and analysis of the operations. Abraham Maslow's "Need Theory" further builds on this concept by arguing that man has a hierarchy of needs starting with the basic physical ones of food, shelter, and clothing, and working through five steps to the intangible needs of self-actualization and fulfillment. These concepts will be further discussed in other chapters.

More recently attention has been paid to the matter of individuals and group behavior in the work situation, and to their relationship in a larger social, cultural, and political system. A topic of current exploration is both the behavior of individuals and groups within organizations and the behavior of organizations as social systems interacting with the environment.

DECISION THEORY SCHOOLS

In the 1950s, 1960s, and into the 1970s contributions have been made to management through disciplines such as mathematics, statistics, and economics (by use of mathematical models for decision-making and prediction, and of game theory and strategies in creative planning); and through psychology and sociology (with theories of leadership and organization, human motivation and behavior, organizational relationships, and nature of authority). This school draws on the common element in all those previously discussed—that being the decision-making aspect. The advent of technology has greatly aided researchers in the development of information systems.

The decision theory school is primarily concerned with the study of rational decision procedures and of the way managers actually reach decisions. Many of the researchers have concentrated on *describing*[11] the decision making process, drawing on psychology and economics, or on *prescribing*[12] how decisions should be made.

The mathematical school, a branch of the decision theory school, is concerned with what to measure and why, with the thought of indicating how best to improve a system or solve a problem.

These management scientists share common characteristics, namely: 1) the application of scientific analysis to managerial problems; 2) the goal of improving the manager's decision-making ability; 3) a high regard for economic effectiveness criteria; 4) a reliance on mathematical models; and 5) the utilization of electronic computers.[13]

This school, as might be suspected, uses techniques such as game theory, simulation, and linear programming in presenting alternatives to the decision maker.

SUMMARY

Very briefly summarized, then, the scientific schools' approach to organization is to study the activities that need to be undertaken to achieve objectives; the human relations approach starts with a study of man's motives and behavior; and the decision theory approach concentrates on the decisions that need to be made to achieve objectives.

All of these schools of management thought are interrelated. All are concerned with the management process, but no one school can begin to provide a comprehensive view. All have strong points and weak points. Some of the best and some of the worst of each can be observed in library operations today.

FOOTNOTES

[1] Larry N. Killough, "Management and the Industrial Revolution," *Advanced Management Journal* (July 1970): 67-70.

[2] Charles Babbage, *On the Economy of Machinery and Manufacturers* (London: Charles Knight, 1832).

[3] Harold Koontz, "The Management Theory Jungle," *Academy of Management Journal*, v. 4, no. 3 (December 1961): 174-175.

[4] Frederick Winslow Taylor, *Principles of Scientific Management* (New York: Harper and Brothers Publishers, 1941), pp. 36-37.

[5] "Shop Management" in Frederick Winslow Taylor, *Scientific Management* (New York: Harper and Row, 1947), p.31.

[6] Edna Yost, *Frank and Lillian Gilbreth* (New Brunswick, N.J.: Rutgers University Press, 1949), p. 262.

[7] Henry Fayol, *General and Industrial Management*, translated by Constance Storrs (London: Pitman & Sons, 1949), p. 22.

[8] Max Weber, *The Theory of Social and Economic Organizations* (New York: Free Press, 1947).

[9] Luther Gulick, and L. Urwick, eds., *Papers on the Science of Administration* (New York: Institute of Public Administration, 1937).

[10] Chester I. Barnard, *The Functions of the Executive* (Cambridge, Mass.: Harvard University Press, 1950).

[11] James March and Herbert Simon, *Organizations* (New York: Wiley, 1958).

[12] Sheen Kassouf, *Normative Decision Making* (Englewood Cliffs, N.J.: Prentice-Hall, 1970).

[13] Richard M. Hodgetts, *Management: Theory Process and Practice* (Philadelphia: W. B. Saunders Company, 1975), p. 113.

READINGS

Barnard, C.I. *The Functions of the Executive*. Cambridge, Mass.: Harvard University Press, 1938.

Fayol, H. *General and Industrial Management*. New York, Pitman, 1949.

George, Claude S., Jr. *History of Management Thought*. 2nd ed. Englewood Cliffs, N.J.: Prentice-Hall, 1972. paper.

Gulick, L., and L. Urwick, eds. *Papers on the Science of Administration*. New York: Columbia University Press, 1937.

Herzberg, Frederick, *et al. The Motivation at Work*. 2nd ed. New York: John Wiley, 1959.

Howard, Paul. "The Functions of Library Management," *Library Quarterly* (July 1940): 315-340.

Koontz, H., and C. O'Donnell. *Principles of Management*. New York: McGraw-Hill, 1964.

Likert, Rensis. *The Human Organization*. New York: McGraw-Hill, 1967.

Maslow, Abraham H. *Motivation and Personality*. New York: Harper and Row, 1954.

Mayo, Elton. *The Human Problems of an Industrial Civilization*. 2nd ed. Cambridge, Mass.: Harvard University Press, 1946.

McGregor, Douglas. *The Human Side of Enterprise*. New York: McGraw-Hill, 1960.

Taylor, Frederick W. *Scientific Management*. New York: Harper and Row, 1947.

2

THE PLANNING PROCESS

LIBRARY PLANNING

One of the most easily avoided activities in libraries, as in many other organizations, is the planning process. This phenomenon exists despite the fact that planning is the most basic function—all other functions must reflect it. Although there are numerous reasons why libraries neglect planning, the main reason is that it is an extremely difficult, time-consuming process that is further complicated by economic uncertainty, shrinking federal, state, and local support and changing societal priorities. Added to this is the fact that many managers resist proper planning. Too many librarians still tend to emphasize current operations at the expense of planning. This resistance to systematic and comprehensive planning is often couched in such phrases as "planning is just crystal-ball gazing in these days of technological change" or "there's no time to devote to planning because we are too busy with the present." Libraries are often now being mandated by the larger institution of which they are a part to develop long-range plans that attempt to anticipate the programs that will be desirable in some future period. These plans, which become the basis for budgeting, include expansions of programs, staffs, materials, and physical plant. For instance, the University of Washington in September 1973 initiated implementation of a formal long-range planning process for the total university system.[1]

Since planning is an effort to anticipate the future and the inevitable changes that come with it, it can be accomplished only by choosing from among possible alternatives. Some libraries have instituted planning committees, and others (mainly large public and academic library systems such as Columbia University Libraries) have created planning offices within the staff structure of the library. These groups are responsible for developing or guiding the development of certain plans, particularly those that are long range in nature. Such groups, with responsibilities clearly defined, are able to perform more intensive investigations and to analyze and coordinate plans more thoroughly. Columbia University Library's Planning Office is administered by the Assistant University Librarian for Planning, with specific objectives to:

1. Provide a direction and framework for library and information service operations which will guide decision making and problem solving.

2. Improve library service, operations and fiscal control through the application of computer technology and management science to library procedures.

3. Ensure the rational and effective development of information services and resources in the context of University academic planning.

4. Permit the anticipation of future resource needs for information service by establishing plans based on present decisions.

5. Bring the skills and experience of University and Libraries staff members into the planning process.[2]

In developing the planning process, several university libraries (22 as of this date[3]) have used the MRAP (Management Review and Analysis Program) technique as a self-study guide; this technique was developed by the Management Studies Office of the Association of Research Libraries.

Because of successful operations that resulted from an over-abundance of funds, librarians have often been led to attribute these successful programs to their own imagination and intuition. Lack of success, however, is often blamed on "circumstances beyond our control" instead of on the lack of planning. Considerations of what planning is and is not will be helpful in developing a planning attitude.

What Is Planning?

Planning is the process of getting an organization from where it is to where it wants to be in a given period of time by setting it on a predetermined course of action. It is deciding what to do, how to do it, when to do it, and who is to do it. Thus, planning consists of making decisions now regarding possible courses of action in light of established missions, goals, objectives, and other available information. Perhaps the most important reasons for planning are to offset uncertainty and change, to focus attention on clearly defined objectives, to gain economical operation, and to facilitate control. To create a planning "attitude" the concept must begin at the top and be implemented through policies, procedures, projects, and programs of the library. A planning document becomes today's design for tomorrow's action, an outline of the steps to be taken starting now but continuing into some future period. The process leading up to the written document should be discussed with the people most concerned. This is an idealistic attitude, of course, because it is not always feasible for everyone to participate in the varied stages of the planning process. However, the whole organization should be, at the least, informed about the plans that are taking shape. It is when this involvement takes place that the greatest commitment will be achieved. If the staff and the funding authorities are in agreement at this basic stage, then it is realistic to expect that the written plan will be used consistently as a guide by all members of the organization.

This planning process, then, forces action on the part of the institution as a whole. Members of the institution must evaluate and set goals and progress towards them.

Planning should be used daily in the mainstream of the library; it is not a process that the manager uses at occasional intervals when he thinks he has time for it. Without daily planning, decisions become ad hoc choices, activities become random, and confusion and chaos often prevail.

Factors in Planning

The planning process can be arbitrarily divided into four elements:

Time

Time is the first element in the planning process. There are two categories of plans with respect to time: long-range and short-term. These categories refer to the span of time over which the plan is effective, starting with the time when the plan is initiated and ending with the time when the objectives of the plan are actually achieved. Long-range, strategic, or master planning necessitates looking at operations of the library in a most critical and comprehensive way, in order to develop a planning network that connects the sub-plans of individual units, departments, and divisions of the library into one master plan. Perhaps the most touted examples of long-range planning are those produced by communist governments in the form of five- to ten-year plans.

Master planning is a concept that is relatively new to libraries and information centers, whether one is considering total university planning, which would affect academic libraries; city planning, which would have bearing on public libraries; school systems planning, which affects media centers; or corporation planning, which might affect special libraries. Many large library and information centers are now involved in the long-range planning process. An example is the "Academic Plan for the Davis Campus 1970-1980"; and the "University of California at San Diego's Long Range Plan to 1984."[4]

Impetus for master planning, a desirable approach for most complex organizations, came primarily after World War II, when "postwar planning" was important to companies in the United States; this was particularly true because technology was changing and becoming more expensive and companies had to be sure of the need. According to Drucker, strategic planning is

> the continuous process of making present entrepreneurial (*risk-taking*) *decisions* systematically and with the greatest knowledge of their futurity; organizing systematically the *efforts* needed to carry out these decisions; and measuring the results of these decisions against the expectations through organized, systematic feedbacks.[5]

Another definition that proves helpful is the one supplied by Steiner, who states that strategic planning is "the process of determining the major objectives of an organization and the policies and strategies that will govern the acquisition, use, and disposition of resources to achieve those objectives."[6]

Most experts agree that long-range plans should reflect programs five or ten years from the present time. One of the most difficult aspects of long-range plans is that they force the librarian to make certain assumptions about the future concerning such things as population trends for higher education or urban centers; or on-going technological changes that are reflected through networks such as the Ohio College Library Center's operations or through bibliographic data bases. Since there is no way of being absolutely certain about the future, the further ahead one plans the greater is the uncertainty. This makes it even more imperative that such written plans receive periodic review, so that certain aspects of the plan can be updated, deleted, or rethought as the library's priorities shift or change completely.

Short-term plans, on the other hand, usually coincide with the accounting year. Examples of short-term plans are next year's budgets or staff work schedules. This type of planning, often called operational planning, reflects the day-to-day operational decisions that need to be made. These plans are much more detailed than the long-range ones and the objectives that are developed are much more specific. The long-range plans are used as general guides, while the short-range plans bring the concept to an operational stage. Since they are more specific and immediate, they do not carry the uncertainty that long-range plans do.

Collecting and Analyzing Data

The second element in planning is collecting and analyzing data—the more pertinent the information available, the better the planning process will be. This step includes systematic collection of data concerning libraries and information centers, their activities, operations, staff, use and users, at a given time and over a given period—in other words, a study of the whole organization and its operation. Techniques for collecting this data are discussed in the chapter on principles of control.

Levels of Planning

All supervisors, whether they are at the upper, middle, or lower levels in the organizational structure, should engage in planning and should be responsible for planning. Involvement of lower echelon personnel in planning has the advantage of getting the practical point of view of those closer to the scene of the operations. Long-range planning is usually carried out primarily by the upper echelon and is general in nature, while short-range planning is usually conducted by middle- and lower-level supervisors. In libraries where committees or planning offices have been created, this hierarchical approach has disappeared and input from all levels is encouraged. It is easy to see the consequence if the two types of plans are not coordinated.

Flexibility

Flexibility—that is, meeting the changing needs—is the essence of good planning. Any planning that is too rigid to accommodate change is an exercise in futility. This is why it is so important to review long-range plans periodically with a thought to revising priorities that may no longer be paramount. In this respect, it is important to be sure that the library's plans remain consistent with those of the larger organization of which the library is a part.

It should be evident from the previous comments that planning is an attitude, a state of mind, a way of thinking. The whole concept of planning is a network of mutually dependent components ranging from an overall plan to technical plans for specific operations.

Planning Techniques

There are many techniques that are important to the planning process but that are often mistaken for the process itself. Four of these are discussed here.

Standards or Guidelines

These have been established by different groups to present the authorities with standards and to act as guidelines for planning. For example, standards developed by the American Library Association are now in existence for most types of libraries and library service, and they are based on actual or known demands for library services. But these are not plans. They are simply a means of differentiating between acceptable and unacceptable service. What each library must do is to develop individual plans based on demands of the library's clientele, using the standards as guidelines. Both human and technical factors are necessary considerations in developing sound standards.

Forecasting

This is an attempt to find the most probably course of events or a range of possibilities. Forecasts are building blocks, or the foundation on which managers can do their own planning, but forecasting is only one part of planning. The whole process of forecasting involves predicting future trends, influences, and developments that may be beyond the librarian's control. Some techniques that have been used in industry are currently being adapted by libraries for use in forecasting. These include the survey approach, which is used in technological forecasting. The Delphi technique is one such tool which is often used. The steps, briefly outlined, are as follows:

1) A panel of experts on the subject (for instance, library funding) is developed.
2) The panel predicts developments over a specified period of time. There is no group interaction; each member works alone.
3) Results of this list of "developments" are then used to draw up a survey that is sent to each panelist for further reaction—refinement, deletion, etc. This process is repeated until the investigator is convinced that no further alternation in predictions will be made. This technique is sure to gain popularity as more libraries become involved in the long-range planning process.

Another technique that has been used to one degree or another in most libraries is that of "Trend Projection." This technique, in its formal approach, graphically plots future trends based on past experience. For instance, the number of volumes put on reserve and the number of times they have circulated during a semester, if plotted on a graph, can show any significant trend. These are only two of the forecasting techniques that can be used by librarians.

Future Decisions

These are not plans. Plans deal not with future decisions but with the future of present decisions—not with what one should do tomorrow, but with what one must do today to be prepared for the events of tomorrow. Often the library planning approach tends toward making plans for something one will decide to do in the future. Such planning makes for interesting reading, but its purposes are moot.

Bound Documents

Such documents are desirable, but planning is not simply a bound document that results from periodic planning sessions. Changes in environment require changes in plans, so there must be flexibility. Planning should be done when a change is needed or because of dissatisfaction with the current process. This change should be accomplished at that moment.

Environment for Planning

Planning is committing library resources—personnel and material—with the best possible knowledge of the future, systematically organizing the effort needed to utilize these resources, and measuring the results of planning decisions through systematic feedback so that needed changes can be effected. In order to establish a climate for planning within the library or information center at least two things are desirable: 1) the entire organization should know the direction, goals, and expectations of the library; and 2) the library and institutional administration should know of all decisions, commitments, and efforts of the organizational members. At this point the library can proceed with a systematic planning process.

Several forces work simultaneously to have an effect on library planning. Both the external and the internal environment influence library planning. For instance, general information on social trends, cultural changes, and political and economic forces is needed if there is to be effective planning of the operations of libraries and information centers. Awareness of national and regional library plans, including cooperative programs and networking, is an important professional factor.

The institutional environment also creates a competitive relationship with other departments in the broader organization, whether these are, for instance, other academic units of the college, university or school; other departments (such as the Department of Parks and Recreation) in a city government; or other units of a business concern of which the special library is a part. Particularly in the light of revenue sharing from the federal government, public libraries must compete for federal support and local attention. This puts a much greater responsibility on the librarian for "selling" programs and being accountable for their outcome.

Future of Library Planning

The immediate problem for library administrators is gaining an understanding of how and why to plan. The first step in improving library services is to recognize all the factors that have been discussed above. The next step is individual planning, which each library must do; and in so doing, it must provide the services that represent the goals of that library. A number of libraries have now developed formal long-range plans that might serve as models. "Tomorrow's libraries will be the result of today's planning." Today's planning, then, must be based on clearly formulated objectives that will encourage all parts of the organization to work toward the same goal. It is a challenge and a responsibility for libraries to be able to integrate resources toward achieving common goals. Setting these goals and objectives is the basic step in developing long-range plans for the library.

OBJECTIVES FOR LIBRARIES

An objective, according to Webster's Unabridged, is that toward which effort is directed; an aim or end of action. Identification of the broad objectives, the service objectives, of a library or information center is the first step in the planning process. One of the difficulties of developing a set of goals and objectives is the confusion that exists in the terminology used; objectives are variously referred to as mission, goals, guiding principles, targets, or purposes. There are probably shades of differences between those terms, but there doesn't seem to be consistency in this interpretation. For instance, the University of Tennessee, in its "Goals and Objectives Statement," defines goals as "statements which are subordinate to objectives and reflect specific measurable steps to be taken," while the University of Washington describes goals as "a long term mission or policy statement describing the direction in which the organization is moving."

Just as planning may be thought of in a hierarchy from strategic or long-range plans to the short-range or operational ones, so the objectives of the library can be indicated in such a hierarchy. The peak of the pyramid consists of the most general, all-encompassing ones, and the lower ones build from that. In the formulation of plans, mission should precede goal, which should precede objectives, if there is to be an integral relationship among them.

Figure 2-1
Objectives Hierarchy

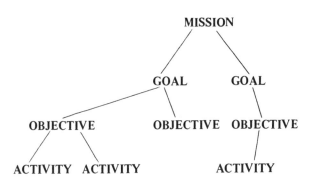

Formulating Objectives

Objectives provide a focus for policy making and for management decisions of all types. "What is the purpose of this organization?" is the first question that must be addressed in the process of setting objectives. After this has been answered, other planning can be undertaken. Of course, libraries and information centers are typically born with service objectives. For public libraries the mission has traditionally been education, information, and recreation, and the library emerged as the vehicle to accomplish this mission. One should take this mission one step further by defining the overlap between the needs of the user and the capabilities of the library or information center. This intersection is the basis of the library's goals. Failure to identify this common ground correctly leads to the selection of goals—and later objectives—that are non-related or unrealistic. Likewise, it must be remembered that objectives are dependent on time and that they are likely to change over a period of time.

All activities and policies should be directed to the achievement of these goals and objectives. Clear objectives also encourage a consistency in management, planning, and decision making over an extended period of time. Unfortunately, objectives often exist in the thinking of management without being made explicit, or at least they are often never verbalized. Such an approach can lead to confusion and discouragement, and a great deal of energy can be expended on faulty assumptions. Objectives should set the pattern for the structure of the organization.

Levels of Objectives

Four distinct levels of objectives can be identified in libraries and information centers.

Broad General Mission

These could be called the "creed" or statement of mission or purpose of the organization. As an example, Cornell University Library states that its mission is "to provide bibliographical, physical, and intellectual access to recorded knowledge and information consistent with the present and anticipated teaching and research responsibilities and social concerns of Cornell."[7] Likewise, Public Law 941, Section 371, states that the purpose of the National Library of Medicine is "to assist the advancement of medical and related sciences, and to aid the dissemination and exchange of scientific and other information important to the progress of medicine and to the public health." The official mission indicates the general purposes of the organization, the mission statement is most often set forth in the charter, annual report, or other authoritative pronouncement of the organization. The mission statement is the justification for the organization's existence.

Organization-Wide Goals

Often referred to as long-range goals of the organization, these are broad aspirations that represent a philosophical basis for the operation of the library. They serve as the basis for development and as measures against which the success or failure of the objectives can be determined. For example, the University of Illinois Library states the following as its goals:

a) Effective organization and administration
b) Adequate financial support
c) Continued rational development of the collections
d) Strong staffing and staff development
e) Quality and efficiency of operations
f) Effective services to users
g) Adequate physical facilities[8]

The University of California at San Diego Library states its goals as follows:[9]

1. To provide a collection and resource materials adequate to support the instructional and research programs.
2. To develop and maintain adequate library facilities.
3. To make the Library's collections and its reference and other public services accessible to faculty, students and staff of the university, and as far as possible, to individuals, public and private institutions, and industries in the San Diego region. In order to meet these goals it is the Library's objective to select, develop, and maintain the qualified staff necessary to provide the collection and services.

Specific Objectives

These can either be departmental objectives or short-range ones for the whole organization. Some objectives are tangible or measurable, while others are not—for instance, one objective may be to improve morale, but how can one measure morale? A real challenge also arises when it is determined that there are multiple service objectives. What, for example, is the major service objective of a university library? Is it to provide needed materials for students at the undergraduate level or is it to provide materials that will allow faculty and graduate students to do research and therefore advance the state of knowledge? Or is it both? Specific objectives can be related to each goal; for instance, the goal may be to develop library collections using general guidelines set down. One specific objective, to use Oklahoma State University's plan as an example, might be

the annual budget for library materials (books, periodicals, binding and other media) should closely approximate the following for the years indicated:

By 1975	—	$600,000
By 1980	—	$800,000
By 1985	—	$960,000[10]

Activities

These more elemental tasks are directly related sub-sets of the objectives. They are usually short-term or repetitive and measurable.

All four elements of the hierarchy of objectives involve: 1) the clients—who they are and who they are not; 2) the services—what services are needed, which should be added, and which deleted; 3) the personnel resources—what professional and clerical skills are needed to provide services; 4) the financial resources—what and where they are and how to get them; 5) the community responsibilities—is the library a social institution?

Unlike business, where the first objective is often to make the highest profit possible, libraries have as one of their primary objectives that of socialization—to pay good wages, to make the organization a good place to work in, to provide a useful service, to attract a competent staff. Libraries, however, are responsible to higher authorities, which to some extent dictate the social objectives. Therefore, objectives of libraries can be forced on them by the community, through social obligations, or by the employees, through collective bargaining or other means. Just as profit and social objectives in business organizations often dictate opposite courses that force a compromise, so in libraries the individual's objectives and those of the organization as a whole can conflict and force compromise.

Setting Objectives

Objectives can be conservative or expansive, but should be such that they "stretch" the enterprise. There is a real danger of setting objectives that are in reality hopes and not attainable end points. In setting objectives many things must be taken into account: the strengths of the library, the limitations of the library, and how much can be accomplished with the resources available and the objectives of the larger institution of which the library is but one part. A balance must be reached between what is obtainable and what is challenging. The greatest problem in planning is bridging the gap between what is desirable (stated objectives) and what is possible (real objectives). The approach to management by objectives has forced organizations to provide an accurate picture of real, actual, operating objectives. Also, because most libraries have multiple goals, management by objectives, a technique to be discussed later, forces the organization to establish each objective in light of the others. They must fit and must be consistent and harmonious.

Improper selection or faulty specifications of objectives will waste planning time and money, will result in frustration, and will make the entire planning activity futile. Every library should spell out its own objectives instead of relying totally on those of other organizations, because these objectives determine the policy, planning, and organizational structure of that library. These objectives represent the end toward which organizing, staffing, and controlling are aimed. The goal of every library is to survive. To do this, it cannot even stand still, let alone decline in vigor. It must produce services that are in demand; therefore, it must state its general objectives in terms that apply to all libraries of a given type, but also in specific terms aimed at service to that particular library's clientele. To say that the objectives of a library are to provide the right book to the right reader at the right time is not enough. It may be more accurate to state its objectives as being: 1) to provide all materials necessary to meet the needs of all patrons; 2) to attract highly qualified staff.

Once a master plan to achieve goals has been developed and approved, the individual objectives are assigned to one or more subordinate units of the organization for execution, and these units in turn assign activities for individual sections of the unit. Ideally, each unit executes several plans simultaneously, making consistent progress toward several objectives but keeping in mind the priorities that have been established. In practice this may not work effectively. Every person seems to invest more time in fulfilling objectives related to his own particular interests, thus he may lose sight of the priorities established by that unit. For instance, the major objective of a catalog department may be to catalog all current, incoming materials. Other objectives (e.g., getting rid of a backlog that may have accrued or reclassifying the already classified collection) may take priority with some staff members—particularly those who are responsible for reclassifying or cataloging the backlog—so that the department falls behind in achieving its major objective. Then, too, unforeseen circumstances arise to unbalance the accomplishment of a group of objectives. The loss of a key person is a good example of something that can jeopardize the achievement of objectives or that can at least force major revisions or delays.

Unfortunately, most people carry out tasks; they do not achieve objectives. Most do not even know the objectives of an organization. Ask any librarian what justifies his position and he will nearly always answer, if the answer is serious, by listing the work that he does, the tasks or machines that he controls or supervises. Each librarian is concerned with the means and methods, and he may not be able to describe the objectives. Perhaps the main benefit of having aims and setting objectives is that it provides a new way of looking at the old job; it concentrates thought and often gives a sense of purpose. Organizations with clear aims and objectives tend to have a higher staff morale. Understanding of objectives and their environment, plus participation, is the best assurance of loyalty to them. By setting written objectives and communicating them to the staff, the organization is encouraging individuals to think through the more logical courses of action and is providing them with a yardstick for activities. Setting objectives is also an excellent way of measuring output for the organization.

Management by Objectives

The process of goal setting involves decision making, choosing from among alternatives. Once established, these goals act as guides or standards both for the organization and for individuals in the decision-making process. One technique that is being regularly used by management in libraries is "management by objectives," which combines individual and institutional goal setting with the decision-making process. Much has been written on management by objectives, a technique that has been in favor with industry and commerce for some time. Peter Drucker, in *Practices of Management*, first pointed out the technique.

This approach involves the establishment and communication of organizational goals, the setting of individual objectives pursuant to the organizational goals, and the periodic and then final review of performance as it relates to the objectives.[11]

Description of the technique has been further refined by Odiorne, who defines it as

a process whereby the superior and subordinate managers of an organization jointly identify its common goals, define each individual's major areas of responsibility in terms of the results expected of him, and use these measures as guides for operating the unit and assessing the contribution of each of its members.[12]

In essence, management by objective means establishing sets of objectives and approaching them as a team over a stated period of time. Objectives must be measurable, with time limits, and they must require specific and realistic action. Management by objectives is perhaps the most evident example of participative management because it involves everyone, to an extent, in the management process.

In this process, at the start of appraisal periods, supervisor and subordinates agree upon specific results to be obtained during this period; they establish what's to be done, how long it will take, and who is to do it. The whole process rests upon several premises:

1)   Clearly stated objectives. If they are not clear, they should be clarified.
2)   A succession of specific objectives. Bench marks must be established to measure progress.
3)   Delegation of specific objectives. Certain people should be responsible for accomplishing specific objectives.
4)   Freedom to act. Subordinates should be presented objectives and authority and then be charged with accomplishment of those specific objectives.
5)   Verifiable results. To achieve objectives, it is best to quantify them. If they are non-quantifiable objectives, they may relate to quantifiable ones. For example, if one wants to reduce absenteeism by 50 percent, then the reasons for absenteeism must be considered. If the reasons relate to morale, then morale must be improved, etc.
6)   Clear communication. This exists only when objectives are specific, are agreed upon by all parties, are budgeted, and are known by all individuals who have a reason for knowing.
7)   Shared responsibilities. Team effort is the key to management by objectives.
8)   Personal accountability. Each person must be accountable for the achievement of his assigned objectives.
9)   Improving management ability. Management is able to plan more objectively when these premises are accepted.

The approach to management by objectives is set in phases of operation: 1) finding the objectives; 2) setting the objectives; 3) validating the objectives; 4) implementing the objectives; and 5) controlling and reporting the status of the objectives. Libraries and information centers are beginning to explore this technique's potential for their operation. The things that must be guarded against are: making the individual's objectives too easy; making them too difficult; setting objectives that conflict with policy; or setting objectives that they hold an individual accountable for something beyond his control.

This concept is expanded in other chapters of this volume.

Finally, objectives, as distinguished from policy, emphasize aims and are stated as expectations; policies emphasize rules and are stated in the form of directions.

POLICY MAKING

In many discourses policy making and decision making are synonomous terms. In actual practice, however, policy making is a part of decision making, in that policies emanate from these original decisions and become general statements or understandings that channel thinking in future decision making. Once policies have been established, they can become effective tools for transferring decision making to lower levels in the organization, because, given the broad policy outline, individuals at all levels can make operational decisions. Perhaps a working definition of policy might be "a verbal, written, or implied overall guide setting up boundaries that supply the general limits and direction in which managerial action will take place."[13]

Both policies and objectives are guides to thinking and action, but there are differences between them. Objectives, as already discussed, are end points of planning, while policies channel decisions along the way to these ends. Another difference is that a policy is usually effective or operational the day it is formulated and continues to be in effect until it is revised or deleted. A policy, then, leads to the achievement of objectives and aids in the decision-making process.

Policy making is not reserved for top management; it is developed at all levels. These levels include, on the one hand, major policies involving all segments of the organization and, on the other, minor policies applicable to only a small segment of the organization. There are many policies in existence in libraries that cover basic directions toward the achievement of the library's stated goals. These include policies relating to the three M's—materials, men, and money (more particularly, the acquisition of materials, personnel appointment and promotion, budgeting, etc.). Examples of library policies might be: 1) all new staff will be rotated through all departments during their first year on the staff (staff development policy); or 2) library materials should present all sides of controversial issues (book selection policy). The kinds of library policies are too numerous to expound here, but policy manuals for all types of libraries enumerate them. Such a policy manual is an important record that is invaluable as a decision-making tool and as a way of communicating within the organization. It is also a basic tool for indoctrinating new staff members.

All libraries have policies, whether they are written or unwritten, sound or unsound, followed or not followed, understood or not understood, complete or incomplete. It is almost impossible to delegate authority and clarify relationships without the existence of policy, since one cannot make decisions without some kind of guidelines. In the absence of policy, each case is resolved on its own merit, so consistency is lacking. Lack of policy means that questions may be considered time after time, by a number of different individuals, with the result that energy is wasted, conflicting decisions are made, and confusion develops. Policy insures some degree of consistency in the operation. Just as with objectives, policies may fall into a general area and be stated in the form of principles that guide the library (these being broad, comprehensive, and basic), while others are specific or operational and deal with day-to-day activities.

Sources of Policy

Sources of policy making fall into groupings that are easily categorized:

1) Originated policy: Policies developed to guide in the general operations of the library. These flow mainly from the objectives and are the main source of policy making within the organization.

2) Appealed policy: Decisions needed by supervisors, in their assigned areas of responsibility, who take it through the chain-of-command where a common law is established. This type of policy can cause confusion because it is forced and often does not have the thorough consideration that is required. To draw an extreme example, it may be

the "forced" policy of the catalog department—for administrative convenience only—to make no more than two subject headings for each monograph. One can imagine the effect this could have on the reference department's work with patrons.

3)   Implied policy: Developed from actions that people see about them and believe to constitute policy. Repetitive actions, such as promotion from within, may be interpreted by subordinates as policy. This may or may not be the case, but particularly in these areas staff must be informed and briefed so that misunderstandings do not arise.

4)   Externally imposed policy: Such policies, which come through several channels, are policies that dictate the working of an institution but that may be beyond its control. For example, laws have a direct bearing on the policies that libraries may formulate. These laws are both general, such as those relating to destruction of public property (Malicious Damage Act 1861), and specific, such as these relating to copyright (Copyright Act 1976). When policies are being formulated the laws must be remembered.

No matter what objectives are set for, say, public libraries, the objectives are also subject to the law. In the case of public libraries, the process of setting objectives must reflect the government's policy on public libraries at the local, state, and national level. If, for instance, for local economic reasons, a local authority decides to spend all library funds on its children's services or, at the other extreme, to close the library down completely—such an action might be in conflict with its obligation and thus illegal. Perhaps a better example might be if a library decides to re-plan its service points, with the result that a branch library is closed down. People living nearby may object and petition their representative. He may decide that such a policy is not securing an improvement and may prevent the authority from carrying out its policy no matter how well-intended it may be.

Another example of library laws relates to finance. An excellent example of this is the set of conditions under which British universities regulate the spending of funds. The Universities Grant Committee's document states very precisely the standards for capital investment, book stock, etc. It states, for example, that library space should be 25 square feet per reader and 60 square feet for each 1,000 books at a cost of 5.37½p. per square foot. Because this is an external control upon all university grant spending, it necessarily affects the planning and administration of the university library.

Levels of Policy

Policies fall into two groups: those that deal with the managerial functions of planning, organizing, staffing, directing, and controlling; and those that deal with the functions of the enterprise, such as selection and development of resources, finance, and personnel and public relations—all of these relating to the characteristic behavior of the library to gain its objectives.

Effective Policy Making

Several basic rules should be considered when policies are being formulated. Some of these may seem simplistic and even redundant, but it is surprising how many organizations ignore these basics when they are formulating policy. To be most effective, policies should be:

1) reflective of the objectives and plans of the organization. The three should dovetail so that each builds on the other instead of working against it.

2) consistent, so that efficiency is maintained. Again, the existence of contradicting policies simply dissipates the desired effect.

3) flexible, so that they can be changed as new needs arise. Many organizations adhere to out-of-date policies. On the other hand, a laissez-faire approach to policy formulation and revision may lead to disillusionment on the part of those who are charged with carrying it out. Therefore, some degree of stability must be maintained. Policies should be controlled through regular and careful review.

4) distinguished from rules and procedures. Rules and procedures are firm, while policies, as guides, allow for latitude in their use.

5) written, so that they are easily communicated to staff. A clear policy, well written, is an aid to information dissemination. Stated policies have several advantages:

1) they become available to all in the same form; 2) they can be referred to so that anyone who wishes can check the policy; 3) misunderstandings can be referred to a particular set of words; 4) they indicate a basic honesty and integrity of the company's intentions; 5) they can more readily be disseminated to all who are affected; 6) they can be taught to new employees more easily; 7) the process of writing forces managers to think more sharply about the policy, thus helping achieve further clarity; and 8) they generate confidence of all persons in the organization in the leadership of top management and in the fact that everyone will be treated substantially the same as the rest under given conditions.[14]

Procedures, Rules and Regulations

A number of techniques are available for carrying out policy. Each of these has some unique aspect.

Procedures are guides to action rather than guides to thinking, and they are subordinate to policies. They establish a method of handling repetitive tasks or problems and may be thought of as measures by which work is performed. Greater efficiency in routine jobs can be achieved through procedures that identify the best way of getting the job done. Procedures tend to be chronological in listing what is to be done. Examples of procedures are: 1) timetable for budget preparation; 2) sequence of steps to be followed in searching and ordering library materials; or 3) interlibrary loan procedures. Procedures are helpful in routine decisions because they break down the process into steps.

The relationship between procedures and policies can be indicated by an example: library policy may grant employees a month's annual vacation; procedures, established to implement this policy, will schedule holidays to avoid disruption of service, will maintain records to assure each employee a holiday, and will provide a means of applying for the holiday.

Rules and regulations, the simplest type of plan, spells out a required course of action or conduct that must be followed. A rule prescribes a specific action for a given situation and creates uniformity of action. A rule reflects a managerial decision for or against action. Like procedures, rules and regulations guide action, but they specify no time sequence. Like decisions, rules are guides, but they allow no discretion or initiative in their application. Examples of rules might be the prohibition of smoking in the library or the fact that reference books do not circulate. Regulations also establish a course of action that is authoritative in nature; failure to adhere to regulations can elicit discipline.

DECISION MAKING

Actual selection from among alternatives is the core of planning. A decision must be made, with a course of action in mind, by choosing the alternative one "thinks" is best. This is not necessarily the alternative that *is* best, because that can be determined only later. Of course, such a choice implies an awareness of alternatives and of the important factors that need to be considered. It is a conscious choice and is a much slower process than one would imagine. The decision-making process involves a blend of thinking, deciding, and acting. The stereotype of finger-snapping and button-pushing fades with systematic research and analysis. Deliberation, evaluation, and thought must be brought into play before a final decision is made. In the generic sense, many decisions are mundane. However, others are of unmeasured consequence and could change the library's course of action. An example might be the decision to open a new branch library. Concentration on the final act obscures the fact that a number of steps were necessary, and the announcement of the decision is only the final step. Although this discussion is primarily about the steps in a "major" decision process, it is important to remember that we all make decisions in our daily life and that most of these decisions, to one degree or another, are reached by the same process discussed here. Some organizational decision-making, which was originally thought of as in the power of the executive alone, is now being delegated to others in the organization. According to Drucker,

> ". . . decision making can no longer be confined to the very small group at the top. In one way or another almost every knowledge worker in an organization will either have to become a decision-maker himself or will

at least have to be able to play an active, an intelligent, and an autonomous part in the decision-making process. What in the past has been a highly specialized function, discharged by a small and usually clearly defined organ—with the rest adapting within a mold of custom and usage—is rapidly becoming a normal if not an everyday task of every single unit in this new social institution, the large-scale knowledge organization. The ability to make effective decisions increasingly determines the ability of every knowledge worker, at least of those in responsible positions, to be effective altogether.[15]

Group Decision Making

The approach to decision making by groups is quite different from individual decision making, primarily because of group dynamics. However, group decision making should follow the same process, the same steps if it is to be constructive. Although techniques of both decision making and participatory management will be discussed in other sections of this volume, it is pertinent to discuss very briefly here the group decision process. Again we are talking about the broad strategies, objectives, etc., that reflect organizational decisions in the library.

There are several advantages to group decision making:

1) Group judgment. The old adage that "two heads are better than one" implies here. Group deliberation is important in identifying alternative solutions to a problem.
2) Group authority. There is a great fear of allowing one person to have too much authority (witness the current trauma in the federal government). Group decisions avoid this problem to an extent. However, it must be remembered that one person must ultimately answer for decisions that have been made. Thus, the role of leadership in the organization is not diminished but changed.
3) Communication. It is much easier to inform and receive input from all parts of the organization through a group. Also, if various interest groups have been represented during the process of making major decisions, there is less resistance to the decisions. Also, communication permits a wider participation in decision making and therefore can have some influence on employee motivation.

There are also distinct disadvantages to the group approach. As Townsend cynically says, a committee developed to make decisions is a group of "unfits appointed by the incompetent to do the unnecessary." More realistically, disadvantages might be:

1) Cost. Group decision requires a great deal of time, and therefore money.
2) Compromise. Group decisions can be diluted to the least common denominator. Pressures of uniformity force compliance. There are two

ways of viewing this problem. The major drawback may be that "majority rules." The desirability of a consensus should not take precedence over critical evaluation in such a situation. On the other hand, a group can prevent an individual from "riding his own hobby horse" by forcing him into line with the thinking of the rest of the group.

3) Indecision. There are delays in reaching a final decision because of the lengthy deliberations required. Groups are often charged with engaging in too much irrelevant talk and not enough concrete action.

4) Power. One individual usually emerges as a leader. This person may be one who is already in a position of influence in the organization. The authoritarian personality of an administrator can be used as a tactical weapon, so that the group process simply becomes one way of minimizing opposition to an action that has already been decided on by that individual. The degree of cohesiveness of the group and the attitudes of one person toward another are important factors in this group process.

5) Authority. One great disadvantage is that groups are frequently used to make decisions that are beyond their authority. This can cause great delay and only enhances a feeling of frustration on the part of members. The responsibility and authority of the group should be clearly set down at the beginning.

This democratic approach of group decision making affects morale, stresses team approach, keeps individuals aware, and provides a forum for free discussion of ideas and thoughts. Librarians have traditionally not demanded a greater voice in decision-making affairs because they have had an "employee" rather than a "professional" orientation. The higher a person is on the administrative scale, the less aware he is of the inadequate opportunities given for staff participation. This is an area of great discussion and disagreement in all types of organizations.

Steps in Decision Making

If goals for the organization are clear, the first step in decision making is to develop alternatives. This step is possible for almost all situations. Effective planning involves a search for these alternatives. If there is only one solution, management is powerless to devise alternatives and no decision is required, although some adjustments may be necessary. In most cases, however, the process may lead to several alternatives, so judgment or opinions become a very necessary factor.

Final selection of a course of action is a matter of weighing expected results against enterprise objectives. What's best for one segment is not necessarily best for the whole. In the example mentioned above, making only two subject cards for the catalog is easier for the cataloging department but harder for the reference department. Choosing a course of action commits the entire enterprise to the chosen position.

The scientific approach to decision making requires that one first identify the problem. Once that has been done, the decision maker must collect and analyze all data that are available on that particular problem. This includes intuition, opinion, and impression in addition to the concrete data that may have been collected or that should be collected before the final decision is made. It may involve techniques that will be discussed under operational research. After all alternatives have been developed, one must select what appears to be the most appropriate alternative. This selection process involves a great deal of risk as well as uncertainty because it is only after the decision has been implemented, that one can tell whether or not it was an appropriate decision. The final step of implementation, then, brings the decision into the "control" aspect of the organization.

Factors in Decision Making

Several factors influence decision making for libraries. For instance, such things as population trends, educational achievement, user and non-user needs, all point to the necessity of a community analysis before final decisions can be made on services to be offered by the library. Selection from among alternatives is made on the basis of:

1) Experience (relying on one's past experience). In this regard, mistakes as well as accomplishments should act as guides. If experience is carefully analyzed and not blindly followed, it can be extremely useful.
2) Experimentation. This approach toward deciding among alternatives is expensive where capital expenditure and personnel are concerned.
3) Research and analysis. Although this is the most general and effective technique used, it may be expensive, and its benefits must be considered by the individual library. However, the approach is probably more beneficial and cheaper in the long run for larger academic, public, and special libraries. Those advantages and disadvantages will be discussed in the section on operational research.

Evaluating the Decision's Importance

Decisions of lesser importance do not require thorough analysis. However, politics are paramount in decision-making, and this is an area that rests largely in the channels of communication. Consideration of the human factor in the decision-making process is very important; acceptance of change is essential to the success of a decision. Those who will be affected by the decision should be told early on—preferably, they should be involved in the decision from the beginning.

A final, practical list of suggestions may facilitate involvement in the decision-making process.

1) Distinguish big from little problems, to avoid getting caught in a situation that is rapid-fire and not effective.
2) Rely on policy to settle routine problems and reserve the big problems for thorough analysis.

3)	Delegate as many decisions as possible to the level of authority most qualified and most interested in handling the problem.
4)	Avoid crisis decisions by planning ahead.
5)	Don't expect to be right all the time; no one ever is.

Decision making is at the heart of any organization. The approach that the librarian takes to decision making and to the involvement of others will determine the directions the library will take in the future.

FOOTNOTES

[1] University of Washington, "The Libraries Planning Guide Adapted from the University of Washington Planning Guide for Fiscal Years 1974-1981" (November 1973). mimeo.

[2] Columbia University, "Detailed Organization Description of the Columbia University Libraries (June 1973)," p. II.3.1. (April 12, 1973). mimeo.

[3] "The Management Review and Analysis Program: A Symposium," ed. by Michael K. Buckland, *Journal of Academic Librarianship* 1, no. 6 (January 1976), p. 14.

[4] University of California, San Diego, "Academic Plan for the Davis Campus 1970-1980" (mimeo); and "UCSD Library—Long Range Plan to 1984" (mimeo).

[5] Peter F. Drucker, *Management* (New York: Harper and Row, 1974), p. 25.

[6] George Steiner, *Top Management Planning* (New York: Macmillan, 1969), p. 34.

[7] Cornell University, "Statement of Mission," Cornell University Libraries (December 19, 1972). mimeo.

[8] University of Illinois, "Statement of Goals and Objectives of the Library of the University of Illinois at Urbana-Champaign" (October 25, 1972). mimeo.

[9] University of California, San Diego, "UCSD Library—Long Range Plan to 1984" (mimeo), p. 2.

[10] Oklahoma State University, "OSU Library Mission Statement and Goals" (February 8, 1972), p. 2. mimeo.

[11] Stephen J. Carrol, Jr., and Henry L. Tosi, Jr., *Management by Objectives* (New York: Macmillan, 1973), p. 3.

[12] George S. Odiorne, *Management by Objectives* (New York: Pitman Publishing, 1965), pp. 55-56.

[13] M. Valliant Higginson, "Putting Policies in Context," in *Business Policy*, ed. by Alfred and Walter Gross (New York: Ronald Press, 1967), p. 207.

[14] Dalton E. McFarland, "Policy Administration," in *Business Policy*, ed. by Alfred and Walter Gross (New York: Ronald Press, 1967), p. 230.

[15] Peter F. Drucker, *The Effective Executive* (New York: Harper and Row, 1966), p. 162.

3

ORGANIZING

Upon the completion of the planning process described in Chapter 2, clearly defined goals and objectives for an organization will have been established and the programs necessary to achieve the goals and objectives will have been determined. Only after this planning process is complete is the process of organizing undertaken. That planning comes before organizing cannot be emphasized too much. To reverse the process is to encourage the development of an organization that will not permit the accomplishment of planned goals and objectives.

WHAT IS AN ORGANIZATION?

An organization is a structure (man-created) that provides a system through which people can perform assigned activities that contribute to the goals, objectives, and programs of the organization. Any activities that do not contribute to the accomplishment of the organization's goals and objectives have no place in the organization.

Since this structure is man-created, it should in no way be considered permanent, fixed, or sacred. Many managers are reluctant to alter an organizational structure once it has been established. This may be due to fear of change or to a failure to recognize that new activities bring new or modified organizational structures. It has been said that most of the organizations existing today were created to meet goals and objectives that no longer exist for those organizations. To impose new goals and objectives on our old organizational structure can only result in inefficiency, duplication of endeavor, and confusion.

An organizational structure that provides for the efficient achievement of the planned goals and objectives is not an easy structure to develop. In an organization consisting of one person, there is no need to develop an elaborate structure. The one person does everything. But as the organization grows from two to more individuals a structure must be established. Even with two people in one organization, a differentiation of activities occurs and a structure emerges.

As the organizational structure gets larger and more people are involved, more complex problems are encountered. Except for the one-person organization, the planned organizational structure must provide an activity-authority environment in which people can work. The organizational process must provide for the identification and grouping of similar or related activities necessary for achieving the organization's goals and objectives; it must permit the assignment of these activities to appropriate units of the emerging organization. It must provide for the coordination of activities under a manager and the delegation of authority and responsibility necessary for the manager to carry out the assigned activities.

Peter Drucker identifies three ways to determine the kind of structure needed for a specific organization: activities analysis, decision analysis, and relations analysis.[1] He emphasizes that only by detailed and thorough analysis of activities can managers determine what work has to be performed, what activities belong together, and where the activities are placed in the organizational structure. Drucker's decision analysis identifies the kinds of decisions that are needed, where in the structure of the organization they should be made, and the degree of involvement of each manager in the decision-making process. In relations analysis, Drucker emphasizes the relationship of the units of the organizational structure and the responsibilities of each manager to the other units as well as the responsibilities of other units to him.

Koontz and O'Donnell summarize the process of organizing as "a process by which the manager brings order out of chaos, removes conflicts between people over work or responsibility, and establishes an environment suitable for teamwork."[2] Implicit also is recognition of the human factor—that jobs must be structured for people, with all their strengths and weaknesses, and that people must be motivated.

The modern, up-to-date organizational structure will provide an environment that encourages easy communication between organizational units so that everyone understands the function and purpose of all units within the structure, and so that any obstacle to performance—be it organizational or personal—can be removed. The modern-day organizational structure will provide a decision-making communications network that will permit the accomplishment of the goals and objectives of the organization.

DEPARTMENTATION

An organization is structured by identifying and grouping similar or related required activities or tasks into departments. To identify similar or related tasks sounds like a simple process. But it becomes more complex when the tasks are examined to determine how they contribute to the organization's goals and objectives. Such grouping of tasks creates blocks of activity-oriented tasks or people-oriented tasks. How the blocks are placed in relation to one another will indicate the true goals and objectives of the organization—which may be different from those originally stated.

Blocks of activity tasks are those that put primary emphasis on process, procedure, or technique. These tasks can vary from the most routine, which require little skill, to very complex tasks requiring extensive ability and knowledge but also conformity with a process, procedure, or technique. People-oriented tasks, which place primary emphasis on human relationships, require the ability to communicate, to guide or direct, and to motivate other individuals.

Most of the older forms of organization put primary emphasis on the activity-oriented tasks. Since World War II, however, it has been recognized that the people-oriented tasks fulfill very important roles in any organization. An example of routine activity-oriented tasks in a library is the task of shelving books or preparing catalog cards; complex activity-oriented tasks might include the selection of books in accordance with a book selection policy or the development of a computer-based program. People-oriented tasks might include the relationship of the reference librarian to the library user, the attitude of the supervisor to subordinates, or the ability of the chief library manager to work with officials in government or academic institutions.

Having identified blocks of tasks, the job of the organizer is to place them together in a logical order. The question "What blocks should be put together or kept apart?" must be answered. Unrelated tasks will be separated. Likewise, the question "What is the proper relationship of the blocks?" must be resolved. Some task blocks will be primary in importance and some secondary. Some will be subservient to larger or primary blocks.

Drucker suggests that it is not as important to identify all tasks that are required in an organization as it is to identify the key tasks. He proposes that any organization design start with the following questions:

> In what area is excellence required to obtain the company's objectives?

> In what areas would lack of performance endanger the results, if not the survival, of the enterprise?

These are questions that libraries have not traditionally asked themselves. Perhaps the answers to these questions will change library organization. At best, these questions are a real challenge to library administrators.

METHODS OF DEPARTMENTATION

Business and industry have generally used six methods to establish departments: 1) numbers, 2) function, 3) territory, 4) product, 5) customer, 6) process or equipment.[4] Libraries have used some of the same methods, but in many cases they have interpreted them differently from industry. Libraries use the following methods for departmentation:

Number

This concept comes mainly from the military, where a designated number of men made a squad, a platoon, a regiment, etc. Only very occasionally do libraries use this as a basis for organization—for example, in a situation such as the moving of a library, where no special skills except a strong back are required. A designated number of individuals are assigned to the moving process according to the method of moving, the distance the items are to be moved, and the timetable for completing the move. This is usually a temporary organizational structure for libraries that is soon eliminated.

Function

In business, organization by function has been widely accepted, and in libraries, too, this method has been extensively used. The functions of circulation, reference, acquisition, readers' advisor, shelving, to name but a few, have historically been the basis of library organization. The grouping of necessary library activities has identified these specific functions. In some of the organizational patterns that have emerged in the last 40 years, some of these functions have been combined to create one department with sub-departments performing related functions.

In the 1930s it was not unusual to have many functional departments working autonomously. In recent years, many of these have been combined into larger units because the assigned activities were related. A good example is the emergence in recent years of the major functional department of Technical Services, which includes many units that used to be autonomous functional departments. Order or acquisitions departments, catalog departments, serials departments, binding departments, and book processing departments, previously autonomous, are now usually combined because their activities are related to the organization's end goal of acquiring and organizing library resources.

Territory

In industry it has been a principle that all activities in a designated territory or area should be grouped together and placed under the direction of a manager. This permitted industry to adapt to local situations as far as the local labor market, local needs and problems, and local production problems permitted. Libraries have also used this principle of territory or area in their organizational structure. Public libraries and school media centers are much concerned about the location of their central facility; public libraries are concerned about the area to be served by their branch libraries, bookmobiles, and storefront libraries. Academic libraries that have branch libraries such as a science library, architecture library, or education library are concerned that these facilities be in the area where the appropriate clientele will be located.

Product

Large industries have used this method for organization because it allows for specialization. Organization by product is particularly prevalent in diversified industries. Libraries basically do not use this standard, though perhaps the product of a print shop (a printed biography, brochure, or a catalog card) might be interpreted as a product.

Customer

Industry has used this method of departmentation to appeal to the needs and desires of clearly defined customer groups. So, too, have libraries. Since the late 1800s, special children's rooms have been provided in public libraries. Also, public libraries have aimed their service at teenagers, blind and physically handicapped, special groups in the community, and, since the late 1960s, the economically or culturally disadvantaged. This has caused special organizational departmentation in the public library. The academic library has used this method when undergraduate libraries were established and when rare book libraries and special collections were developed for the researcher.

Process or Equipment

Industry has used this standard when large installations have been required—a smelting plant, a steel mill, etc. Libraries have used it, too, but on a much smaller scale. Those libraries that operate a book bindery centralize all the special, heavy binding equipment in one place. But generally this method has been used as a basis for centralizing such smaller equipment as printing equipment, microform readers, phonodisc players, cassettes and films. There is a trend in school media centers and some public libraries to distribute this type of equipment throughout the library and to disregard this method of organization.

Libraries have developed two other methods on which the organizational structure is based:

Subject

Large public and academic libraries use this method extensively today. It provides for more in-depth reference service and reader guidance, and it requires a high degree of subject knowledge on the part of the staff. There is no set pattern that determines the subjects to be included in a subject department. In academic libraries subject departments are usually broad in scope and include all related subjects in such areas as humanities, social sciences, science, etc. In large public libraries more popular titles are used for subject departments. Also, the number of subject departments created in a library varies. There was a period during the late 1930s and early 1940s when major libraries created as many as twelve subject departments in one organization. But, because of the financial problem of staffing so many departments, the present tendency is to create four to six subject departments in one public library.

Forms of Resources

Libraries have frequently used the form in which the resources have been issued as a basis for organization. It is not unusual to find a map department, a film library, a periodicals department, and a documents department as part of the library organizational structure. Large academic and public libraries tend to separate by form, whereas smaller libraries try to incorporate the various forms into broader departmentations.

Only in the most specialized library would a single one of these organizational methods be used; a library usually uses several of the methods. A large public library generally has a circulation department (function), subject departments (combining several functions), branch libraries (territory), children's services (clientele) and perhaps service to business (customer), a print shop (equipment), documents collection (form), etc. Academic libraries also use various methods in setting their organizational structure.

Figure 3-1 shows how even the smallest one-room library uses various methods in its organization.

Figure 3-1
One-Room Library

Much emphasis has been placed on the identification and grouping of tasks to create departments and sub-departments. But one more element is essential in the creation of an effective departmentation for an organization. To each department or sub-department a manager is assigned to whom adequate authority is delegated to permit him to carry out assigned tasks. If a manager in an organization is assigned the responsibility for the accomplishment of designated tasks and the supervision of employees, he must have the authority guarantee efficient performance.

THE SCALAR PRINCIPLE AND THE HIERARCHY

As departments and sub-departments are assigned various tasks, primary and secondary units of the organization emerge. Primary organizational departments are those that have numerous tasks and broad responsibilities; secondary or sub-departments are those that have more specific tasks and more limited responsibility. A sub-department is usually attached to a primary department because its tasks contribute to the fulfillment of the responsibilities of the primary department. The manager of the primary department supervises the manager of the sub-department to assure compliance with the needs of the primary department. Authority, therefore, flows from the primary to the secondary supervisor.

The scalar principle requires that there be a final, ultimate authority in every organization, and that lines of authority extend downward through the organization to every subordinate position. The clearer the line of authority, the more effective will be organizational performances and communication. Henry Fayol described the scalar principle as

> ... the chain of supervisors ranging from the ultimate authority to the lowest ranks. The line of authority is the route followed—via every link in the chain—by all communications which start from or go to the ultimate authority. This path is dictated both by the need for some transmission and by the principle of unity of command, but it is not always the swiftest. It is even at times disastrously lengthy in large concerns, notably in governmental ones.[5]

A clear understanding by each subordinate in the line of authority or, in military terms, in the line of command, is necessary for effective organizational functioning. He knows to whom he is responsible and for what; further, he knows the parameters of his authority in relation to other employees.

As a result of the ranking of organizational units, a hierarchy develops. A hierarchy is defined as "any system of persons or things ranked one above the other."[6] The concept of the hierarchy has existed for centuries. While much of the development of this concept can be attributed to the military, it is the Roman Catholic Church that developed the concept as an efficient organizational device.[7]

A hierarchy is usually illustrated as a triangle with the ultimate authority at the apex of the triangle and authority flowing downward to all other parts of the triangle.

In an effective organization, the position holding ultimate authority will delegate authority to subordinate managers. The delegation of authority to subordinates does not mean that the final authority relinquishes that authority. A major supervisor is responsible for the actions of his subordinates even if authority has been delegated. What actually has happened in many libraries is that the responsibility to perform designed activities has been assigned to a subordinate, but the authority to accomplish those designed activities has been withheld. Many administrators are afraid to delegate authority; they clutch it tenaciously. But a subordinate given responsibility without authority is in a difficult position and probably will not be able to function efficiently.

Thus, while the historical concept of the hierarchy centralized all authority in the primary administrator (be he king, commander, or Pope), the current concept is that the primary administrator must delegate sufficient authority to a subordinate to permit him to accomplish assigned activities and responsibilities. Authority should be delegated downward to that place in the organization where decisions need to be made. This results in a decentralization of authority in place of the traditional centralization of command.

LINE AND STAFF

Line positions, those having authority and command in an organization, are the decision makers of the organization. Another type of position exists in many organizations. Staff positions are advisory positions without authority. The concept of staff also developed from the military. It is said that Alexander perfected the staff concept during his conquest of Macedonia. The Catholic Church organization utilizes staff services in its central administration through the Sacred College and the Roman Curia.[8] Both institutions are regarded as advisory to the Pope, who delegates no authority to them and is not obligated to accept their advice.

Sometimes a staff unit is defined as one that deals with "ideas." But it is broader than that. In today's organizations, a staff unit may be a research unit, a personnel office, a public relations office, or a systems analyst. The important concept is that the unit has no authority; it functions in an advisory capacity only. The manager of a staff unit is supervised by a superior and in turn may supervise subordinates within the staff unit. But nowhere does he have authority over the organization.

A library personnel office, for example, may have the responsibility of receiving applications, interviewing applicants, maintaining personnel files, recommending promotion, transfer, etc. But he does not have the authority to cause any of these actions to take place. Only the line position—the authority position—can take action.

But staff positions in an organization are extremely important. They provide the facts, the information needed by the decision makers. They are the individuals skilled in specific functions and they apply their skill as a basis for action.

UNITY OF COMMAND

Organizations often to have too many bosses. The organizational structure should guarantee that each employee is supervised by only one supervisor. Only one supervisor should make assignments and access the success of the employee in achieving those assignments. Too often, however, in business and in libraries, employees have several supervisors. In libraries, this is particularly true of the clerical staff and shelvers. When more than one supervisor supervises an employee, the employee is placed in the awkward position of determining whose work to do first, the style in which the work is wanted, and which instruction to follow. The principle of unity of command protects the employee from undesirable situations that result from dual or multiple supervision.

SPAN OF CONTROL

The phrase "span of control" is well entrenched in management thought. And it is an important part of management. But the word "control" may be misleading. This phrase really raises the question of how many individuals one supervisor can supervise well. "Control" might better be replaced by "management," for the concept concerns the number of supervisors that one manager can manage efficiently.

There are no established criteria to resolve this problem, and in actual practice the number of supervisors assigned to one manager varies extensively— usually from five to nine. But there are situations where many more than nine supervisors are assigned to one manager.

One of the criteria used to determine the number of people one manager can adequately manage concerns the kind of assignment given the various supervisors. If the activities of the various units assigned to one supervisor are similar, then perhaps the number can be increased; if the activities vary extensively and require a thorough knowledge of a great variety of activities, the number should be decreased. One must consider the knowledge the manager must have to do an adequate job of managing. The broader and more detailed the required knowledge, the fewer the number of assigned units there should be.

Another criterion concerns the amount of time involved in communication. Time is becoming a critical element in many enterprises. A good manager who has a number of supervisors to supervise will try to reduce the time necessary for the supervising. He will spend more time in the initial training of a new supervisor, will give assignments in broad terms of goals or objectives to be achieved, and will delegate authority to permit the supervisor to supervise his personnel. If the span of control is large and the manager fails to function as described, his time will be consumed by frequent conferences, daily meetings, and repetitive instruction. He will not use his time efficiently.

When one manager has many organizational units reporting to him, a flat or horizontal organization is created and he has an extensive span of control. There are few levels of operation in a flat organization.

Figure 3-2 shows only two levels of operation—the director and the supervisor of each unit to which specific activities have been assigned. But the scope of knowledge required of the director is extensive, indeed. While time would be saved because of the absence of many levels, the amount of supervision given each unit would probably be minimal.

Figure 3-2
Flat Organization

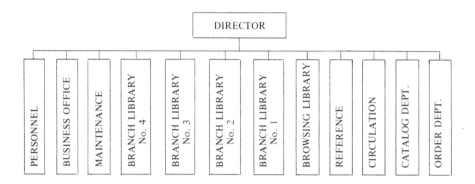

As related units are put together under one supervisor, a vertical organization is created and the span of control is reduced. Figure 3-7 (page 62) shows a vertical organization with four levels of operation. Each supervisor's span of control is small, except for the director, who has six people to supervise—a great reduction from the fourteen people shown in Figure 3-3 (page 59).

The principle of span of control is that there is a limit in each managerial position to the number of persons an individual can efficiently manage. But that number must be determined by the variety of activities assigned and the amount of time a manager can give to each subordinate supervisor.

FUNCTIONAL AUTHORITY

Functional authority is that supervisory power exercised on the unit by a position outside the organizational unit. Seldom is functional authority assigned by a major manager; rather, it emerges as the outside position operates in the organizational unit. While the outside power may be another line supervisor, more frequently a staff position is involved. It is dangerous for an administrator to permit the development of functional authority, since it violates the principle of unity of command.

When line supervisors need assistance that requires special knowledge, it is easy for the specialist, the staff position, to receive permission from the administrator to assist the line supervisor. Gradually this "permission" translates itself into authority. Such action erodes the authority of the major supervisor. While such authority is usually limited to "how" (and occasionally "when") action is to occur, it generally does not influence the "where, what, and who" aspects of personnel assignments.

The main supervisor may ask the library personnel officer to explain grievance procedures to a line supervisor. That request gradually changes to authority over the line supervisor in matters relating to grievances. Functional authority develops as the line supervisor accepts the direction of the staff officer in place of the primary supervisor's direction.

In libraries, functional authority frequently develops in the area of the specialists who work with children, young adults, and adults. Frequently these specialists are called "coordinators." Regardless of their title, they are expected to work with employees who perform their type of specialty. Thus, the coordinator of work with children will be expected to train the children's librarian in public branch libraries. At the same time, the head of the branch library expects to do the same thing. So the coordinator is exercising functional authority and the branch librarian is exercising line authority—to the detriment of the children's librarian, who is caught in the middle.

In order to avoid internal conflicts, the role of the individual exercising functional authority needs to be clearly defined. All parties must understand the parameters within which the individual exercising functional authority operates.

ORGANIZATIONAL POLICIES

In order to maintain consistency and continuity, written organizational policies should be prepared as the organizational structure is established. Of course, any changes in the structure will require changes in the policy statements.

The establishment of organizational policies helps to meet the requirements of the *principle of functional definition*. This principle establishes the concept that the more a position, a department, or any unit of an organization understands and has a clear definition of its authority and responsibility, the results expected, and its relationship to other organizational units, the better will the individuals concerned respond, and the better will be their performance.

A policy may be defined as a statement that guides present and future action. It is a general statement that guides the action of employees in the decision-making process. It is true that policy has a restrictive effect on the decisions employees may make. But such policies assure compliance with the organizational structure which has been created to achieve goals and objectives.

A policy is a public statement. It is available to all employees and is discussed with them to assure understanding. Employees should not have to try to identify organizational policy from the action or occasional statements of the manager.

Organizational policies should include the following:

1) Statements identifying the laws that authorize the establishment of the library. Libraries may operate under state law, county or municipal

ordinances, or charters. All types of libraries (except special libraries operated by private industry or incorporated bodies) have a legal base for their operation.

2) Statements describing the departmentation that has been established as the organizational structure. The tasks and responsibilities of each unit—the large organizational unit as well as each sub-unit—must be defined. The relationship of one unit to another is established by describing the chain of command (line of authority). Statements describing activities and responsibilities naturally limit the scope of activities of the various organizational units.

3) Statements describing the resources of the organizational unit. In libraries it is possible to list the classification numbers for which a department is responsible or to identify the types of resources to be housed in that unit. For example, a fine arts department may be responsible for all books in the Dewey Classification 700. That department is responsible for the selection of all titles and for the replacement, duplication, and weeding of these resources. In addition, the department is assigned responsibility for maintaining a picture file, a phonodisc collection of classical and popular recordings, and a collection of large art prints. Because librarians tend to develop special indexes, it is wise to identify the authorized indexes that will be maintained by the department.

The purpose of such organizational policy statements is not to limit the creativity of the staff but rather to assure consistency in the operation of the organizational structure. Such policy statements also provide an excellent method of communicating to the employees the responsibility of each organizational unit other than the one to which they are assigned.

ORGANIZATIONAL CHARTS

An organizational chart is a graphic presentation of the organizational structure. Although it includes staff units, primarily it shows how departments are tied together by lines of authority. Lines of authority are solid lines; lines that show staff organizational units are broken lines. Formal communication follows the lines of staff and authority. Informal lines of communication are generally not shown on the traditional organization chart.

On an organization chart, authority flows down and out. It does not return to the original line of authority. For example, in Figure 3-3, the main line of authority flows from the director down to the assistant director and from him down and out to the three functional departments.

In Figure 3-3, the business office is supervised by the director only. Authority flows from the director down and out to the business office and stops there. The business office has no authority over the assistant director or over other organizational structures shown in Figure 3-3. An understanding of the principle that authority flows out and stops is very important in interpreting organization charts.

Figure 3-3
Organization Chart Showing Authority Lines

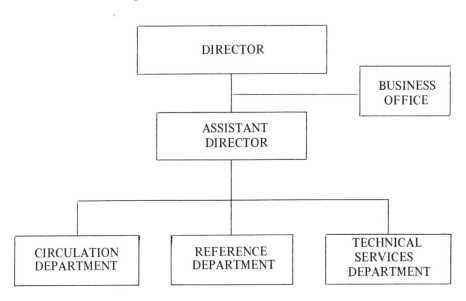

Figure 3-4 illustrates an organization that has both line and staff organizational units.

Figure 3-4
Line and Staff Organizational Units

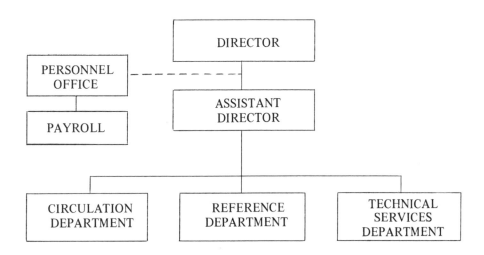

The director has authority over the personnel officer. His authority goes down and out the broken line. The personnel office serves in an advisory capacity to the director and to all other units of the organization, without authority over any unit. However, the personnel office, in its own internal operation, has line authority in that it supervises the payroll functions.

Some of the blocks in Figures 3-3 and 3-4 seem to represent individuals (i.e., director and assistant director), while others represent functions (i.e., circulation, reference, and technical services). The blocks representing functions include all assigned activities and a manager. The blocks that seem to represent individuals actually represent all the activities assigned to that organizational unit. For the director, activities would include the direct supervision of the business office in Figure 3-3 and the personnel office in Figure 3-4. But, in addition, it is also expected (in both charts) that the director will perform such activities as planning, working with outside groups, organizations, and individuals (such as public library board or the vice-president for academic affairs in a university library), and evaluating library services. The assistant director in both charts would be responsible for day-to-day supervision of the three operating units. But other activities would also be assigned to this organizational unit. Although it may appear that a unit of the organizational structure is designated by an individual's title, one must recognize that the organizational block includes all the activities of that position.

Not all organizations are as simple as those represented by Figures 3-3 and 3-4. Some become very complex. As a result, various means have been developed to show the authority relationship of one unit to another. If the function assigned to reference in Figure 3-3 were expanded, that expansion might be shown as in Figure 3-5.

Figure 3-5
Organizational Chart Showing Two Sub-Units of a Department

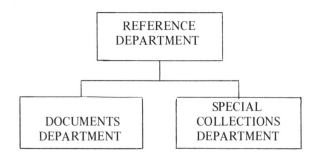

The added organizational units (both by type of material) are equal in status in that they are both immediately supervised by the manager of reference. This same relationship might be charted as follows:

Figure 3-6
Alternative Method of Showing Equal Sub-Units

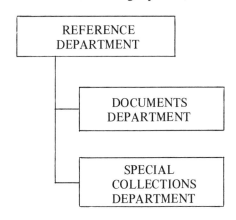

In Figure 3-6, authority flows down from the manager of reference, out to the documents department, and then stops. It continues to flow down and out to special collections and stops. Thus, Figure 3-6 presents a vertical method of showing equal units, while Figure 3-5 uses a horizontal method.

Sometimes the status of an organizational unit is misunderstood because of its location on the organizational chart. The belief is frequently held that the higher on the chart the unit is represented, the greater are its status and authority. This is not true. The importance of an organizational unit is determined by the line of authority and the number of managers that authority passes through before reaching the final authority.

Following the line of authority in Figure 3-7 reveals that the assistant director provides immediate supervision to circulation, reference, and technical services. It is also apparent that these organizational units are important organizational units because they are placed rather high on the organization chart. But what of extension—the unit that provides service outside the central building? It is shown low on the chart. But analyzing the authority line reveals that extension is equal in status, rank, and importance to the other three units. Extension reports to the same position—the assistant director—as do circulation, reference, and technical services.

Figure 3-7
Vertical Organization Chart Showing Placement on a Chart
(Figures in parentheses indicate level according to authority lines)

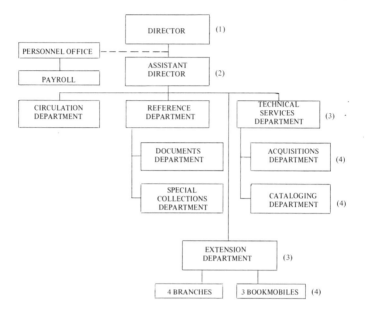

The organization charts presented above are the traditional type. They are all based on the hierarchical concept and are designed to show the relationship of one organizational unit to another through lines of authority. The development of an organization chart will help the manager identify problems or inconsistencies in the organization. One common inconsistency readily identified is the assignment of unrelated or dissimilar activities to a unit. Also, through the analysis of an organization chart the span of control of each supervisor can be determined, and any problems of dual supervision can be readily detected.

Every library, regardless of size, should have an organization chart. It should be available to all staff so that they will understand relationships within the library. But it must be recognized that organization charts are limited in what they can do. While an organization chart can show formal relationships, informal relationships and communication lines between units are not shown. An organization chart shows lines of authority, but at no place does it show the degree of assigned authority. That will have to be described in organizational policies.

Occasionally, the creation of an organization chart may tend to freeze an organization. This can happen particularly under poor leadership. But if leadership is strong and if the organization is dynamic, the organization chart and organization will change. Four factors can cause organization to change:

1) Change in property—the development of new buildings and facilities
2) Change in program—a change in goals and objectives and programs to achieve objectives

3)   Change in techniques—the introduction of mechanization or automation
4)   Change in financial support—the sudden increase or reduction of income

Figure 3-8 shows the organization of the Denver Public Library in 1975. The City Librarian had a span of control of seven positions. While the functions of each of the seven positions varied greatly, the organizational pattern represented a manageable structure. The Director of Public Services was responsible for the largest number of organizational units. Ten different units reported to this Director. Some of the units were based on the principle of location (geographic), some on the clientele being served, and a few on the organizational concept of function. The Assistant Director for Public Services had a span of control of eight. Four of the organizational structures were designed to emphasize subject and the other four function. The Director of Community Services had an interesting group of assigned organizational structures. Of the six units assigned, this position functioned as a staff (advisory) officer to two—the Denver Public Library Foundation and the Friends of the Denver Public Library. Both of these units were incorporated bodies under the laws of the State of Colorado, and they functioned according to their articles of incorporation. The Director of Community Services, therefore, served as a coordinator and advisor to these groups.

In 1976 budgetary restrictions caused a change in the organization. It happened that the position of Director of Public Services was vacant and frozen. Thus, due to the budgetary crisis, it was eliminated. Figure 3-9 illustrates how adjustments were made. The City Librarian's span of control increased from seven to fourteen, representing a variety of organizational patterns—clientele, location, and function. The number and diversity of the units are more than one supervisor should try to manage.

There was also a drastic increase in the number of organizational units assigned to the Assistant Director of Public Services for supervision. In 1975 this position supervised eight organizational units; in 1976 it increased to twelve. The diversity of knowledge required to supervise four broad subject departments, four special libraries (counting the County Jail Library as a special library), and four organizational units structured by function is almost more than can be expected of one supervisor.

The effectiveness of the 1976 organization will depend on the degree of authority and responsibility delegated by the major supervisors to middle management. Each middle management supervisor will have to have a clear understanding of the goals and objectives not only of the total library, but also of each organizational unit. Each must be willing to assume responsibility for the operation of his department. Without such delegation, the total library operation could be in jeopardy.

Figure 3-10, showing the organizational structure of the University of Massachusetts, presents a clear picture of organization by function. No one position has too large a span of control, generally related functions are grouped together, and all lines of authority are clearly delineated. An interesting feature of this chart

Figure 3-8
Organizational Chart
Denver Public Library, 1975
Reproduced with permission

Figure 3-9
Organizational Chart
Denver Public Library, 1976
Reproduced with permission

Figure 3-10
Library Organization Chart, University of Massachusetts
January 1976

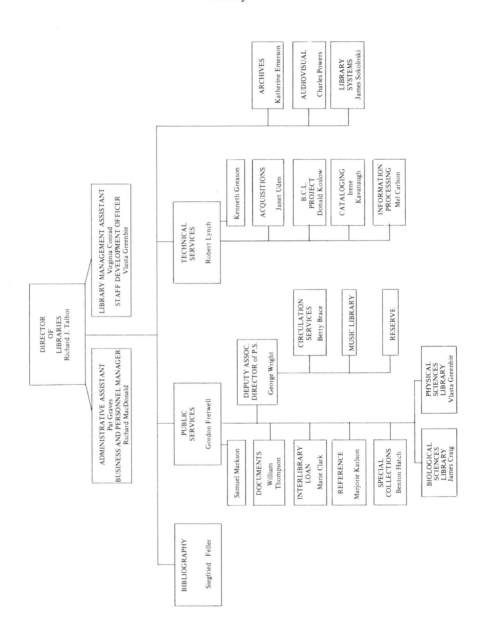

is the inclusion of the primary supervisor's name. This enables staff members to identify immediately the individual having authority and responsibility for the assigned functions.

At times an organization chart similar to Figure 3-10 will include the number of authorized positions and the job classification of those positions. For example, in Figure 3-10 the notation for the organizational unit responsible for circulation services could also show that one professional (1-P), two paraprofessionals (2-PP), and ten clerk positions (10C) were authorized. The organizational chart then assumes the additional function of serving as a manning chart. A manning chart (or table, as it is called in the military) shows the rank and number of positions assigned to a specific organizational unit.

CURRENT TRENDS IN ORGANIZATION
AND ORGANIZATIONAL CHARTS

The organizational process described above represents the historical and traditional method of organizing. However, different companies, industries, and libraries are testing new or modified methods of organization. These new forms basically retain the concept of the hierarchal triangle with the major authority at the top, though some patterns of organization have replaced the individual at the top with an "executive committee," which has final authority.

Odiorne identifies several of these modifications in organization processes. These modifications are based on the assumption that most employees in an organization can perform as they see fit as long as such action is not specifically prohibited by policy and as long as such action contributes to the organization's goals and objectives. He defines the following new management processes:[9]

Bottom-up Management

This process is achieved by delegating authority and the power of decision-making to the lowest possible point in the organization. This delegation of authority supposedly increases employee initiative and requires that employees in the lower echelons of the organization accept more responsibility for their actions.

Collegial Management

This concept, which affects only the top decision maker, has already been mentioned. Instead of a single· final authority position, a group of individuals participate in the making of those decisions that affect the total organization. This structure not only brings more expertise into the decision-making process, but it also gives more individuals a feeling of responsibility.

Project Management

The chart for this concept of organization may look like many small organizational units attached to one another by lines of authority. Odiorne compares it to a bunch of grapes.[10] Each unit has a specific temporary task to perform and, when the task is completed, the group working on a specific project return to their primary job. This structure is widely used; the term "task force" is frequently used to identify the temporary organizational unit assembled to do a specific temporary project, but the terminology does not change the basic concept of organization.

The Doughnut

This method of illustrating an organizational pattern consists of a series of concentric circles, each of which shows a different level of operation. Top administrators are shown in the center and the levels of organization are represented by the successive circles. This is not a change in organizational structure but rather a different way of showing the organization. (See Figure 3-11).

Figure 3-11
An Organizational Chart Presented as a "Doughnut"

The Matrix

Some libraries are developing packages of information for specific community groups. In order to have representative resources and services from all organizational units of the library, it is necessary to create a matrix, a lateral slice across autonomous units. For example, the matrix might consist of the organizational unit responsible for services to the disadvantaged. The creation of a matrix structure might be temporary. But it is very important that the administrators of the autonomous units affected understand what is happening and cooperate with the endeavor. Without this understanding and cooperation, it is possible that the organizational principle of unity of command might be violated.

Regardless of new methods of illustrating organizational structure and new patterns of organization, the basic concept of the hierarchical structure is expected to remain. Managers will still be assigned responsibility and the authority to fulfill that responsibility. Possibly new criteria for structuring the organization will emerge. Drucker suggests four criteria for organizational structure:

1) Result-producing activities—activities which produce measurable results which can be related ... to the results and performance of the entire enterprise,

2) Support activities—[activities]—which while ... essential do not produce direct results,

3) Hygiene and housekeeping activities—activities which are truly ancillary,

4) Top-management activities— ... activities that are the conscience of an organization. The conscience function of giving vision, of setting standards, and of auditing performance against these standards is basically a top-management function.[11]

New trends, such as "management by objectives" and "participative management" are not changes in the basic concept of organization. Rather, they represent the "humanistic school's" approach to management.

EVALUATION OF AN ORGANIZATIONAL STRUCTURE

Even though the process of organization has emerged over the years and some principles have been evolved, no one would claim that they are infallible laws. Rather, these principles are "truths of general application"[12] by which any organization can be evaluated.

In 1952, the American Management Association found through a survey that most companies used nine criteria to evaluate their organizational structure.[13] Since that time additional criteria have been identified; at the present time, fifteen criteria—stated as principles—can be applied to an evaluation of an organization.[14]

Principle of Unity of Objective

The structure of an organization is effective if all and every unit of the organization contributes to the accomplishment of the organization's goals and objectives.

Principle of Efficiency

The structure of an organization must not only be effective but must also be efficient. To be efficient the organizational structure must make it possible for every organizational unit to contribute its maximum endeavor toward the accomplishment of goals and objectives, without any unsought consequences or costs.

Principle of Span of Control

Each managerial position can manage a limited number of persons, but the number will vary according to the diversity of activities assigned and their impact on the time required for effective management.

The Scalar Principle

When the line of authority from the ultimate authority to each subordinate position is absolutely clear, effective decision making and organizational communication will result.

Principle of Delegation

The amount of authority delegated managers should be efficient for him to achieve assigned responsibilities.

Principle of Responsibility

The subordinate is totally responsible to his superior for authority delegated, and the superior cannot escape responsibility for the activities of his subordinate.

Principle of Parity of Authority and Responsibility

The responsibility for actions taken under delegated authority cannot be greater than the authority delegated.

Principle of Unity of Command

An individual should report to only one superior.

The Authority Level Principle

An individual manager is required to make decisions according to the authority delegated to him, and such decisions will be referred upward in the organizational structure.

Principle of Division of Work

An organizational structure assigned a group of activities that are necessary to achieve goals and objectives should identify and group similar or related tasks into departments, thereby creating a series of interrelated roles that fit the capabilities and motivations of people. The principle of division of work, which permits broad grouping of tasks, should not be confused with occupational specialization, which allows for specialized and limited tasks only.

Principle of Functional Definition

If a position or a department has a clear understanding of expected results, activities assigned, amount of authority delegated, and informational relationships with other positions, individuals can contribute more adequately to the accomplishment of goals and objectives.

Principle of Separation

If an organizational unit is designed to be a check on the activities of another organizational unit, the individual in charge of the checking unit cannot perform his responsibility if he reports to the unit whose activity he is to evaluate.

Principle of Balance

A balance must be maintained in the application of organizational principles so that an effective structure evolves that permits the accomplishment of goals and objectives. In complex situations, not all principles will have the same priority, nor will they all pull in the same direction. Often varying situations will require one principle to be emphasized more than another until the environment or situation changes.

Principle of Flexibility

Because of changing environments, the more provision made for building in organizational flexibility the more adequately can the organization fulfill its purposes. In a culture that is shifting rapidly, it is essential that an organization be able to adapt to change not only rapidly but efficiently.

Principle of Leadership Facilitation

The organizational structure and authority delegation within it should provide an environment for efficient leadership performance.

ORGANIZATIONAL RENEWAL

Both in industry and in libraries, organizations develop into structures that deter the achievement of desired goals and objectives. Recent industrial history shows that some larger organizations that expanded to meet the needs of World War II production were not able to adjust to changes required by the post-war era. The same structure, procedures, and rules appropriate for a large organization were retained even though the company had to reduce its size and the scope of its activities. Libraries have faced similar problems of adjustment. Having grown fat on federal grants, some libraries have not been able to adjust to the recent lean years of reduced or withdrawn federal funds.

All organizations need a high degree of stability. It is important that in spite of current trends and socio-economic movements, organizations keep sight of their primary goals, and that they have the stability to adapt to change without losing their basic thrust. Libraries usually have a high degree of stability even in times of economic stress. But some libraries are not able to adapt programs or eliminate tasks that in the long view are detrimental to their basic goals.

Stability is not rigidity. A library that has stability is able to adapt to new situations. A library that is rigid in its organizational structure is brittle and may break when change is required. Rigidity develops partly because of the attitudes of the managers and employees toward change. The existing structure is familiar and comfortable and the work habits and processes are personally satisfying and secure.

But other factors also encourage organizational rigidity. Large bodies of policies, procedures, and rules have been developed that prohibit the employees from exercising any initiative or judgment. Every action is dictated by recorded directions. The employee becomes literally frozen by the existence of those guidelines which were originally designed to be a positive force for the organization. It is not uncommon for chief managers to pull back any authority which they might have delegated. An authority-centered organization prevents any decisions from being made except by the chief manager. Actual situations have been observed where large libraries operated under a strong authority-centered librarian. These libraries were so rigid in their compliance with written directions and the inability to make decisions where and when they needed to be made that the libraries literally ground to a halt. The organization was inoperable.

When a library becomes rigid in its organizational and operational structure, the general trend of the employee is either to accept the situation passively, to revolt and leave, or to unionize. Particularly in libraries, the attitude of the employee is to become arrogant toward the user. More concern for compliance with rules is demonstrated that concern for service. In reality, the organization is functioning more to meet its own needs than it is to fulfill its valid goals and objectives.

An organization operating in this manner is a bureaucratic organization serving itself. But an organization need not remain ineffectual, frozen, and rigid. An organization can be brought back to productive life and can return to the dynamic role that its founders envisioned. John W. Gardner, when he was president of the Carnegie Corporation, said "Most ailing organizations have developed a functional blindness to their own defects. They are not suffering because they can't *solve* their problems but because they won't *see* their problems."[15] He proposed nine steps for organizational renewal:[16]

1) There must be an effective program for the recruitment and development of talent. The organization must not only bring in highly talented and motivated people but it must also have a constructive career development program for its present employees.

2) There must be a hospitable work environment for the employee permitting him to feel a part of the organization rather than just a cog in its operation.

3) There must be built-in provisions for self-criticism. Most executives cannot trust themselves to be adequately self-critical. An atmosphere must be created wherein anyone with critical comments will not be afraid to speak up.

4) There must be flexibility in the organizational structure. While specialization and division of labor are at the heart of modern organization, the complex modern organization must constantly be examining its structure.

5) There must be an adequate system of internal communication. Ideas, the product of the human brain, must be examined, evaluated, and judged through a good communication system.

6) There must be a way of combatting the process by which employees become the prisoner of their procedures. Evaluate and eliminate unnecessary rules, procedures, and policies.

7) There must be a method of combatting the vested interests which develop in every organization. At every level there are vested interests and any change threatens someone's special interests, privileges, authority, or status. Everyone's overriding special interest is the continuing vitality of the organization, regardless of vested interests.

8) The concern of the organization must be what it is going to become, not what it has been. It is the future strength and vitality of the organization which is of concern and not past successes.

9)   Organizations are successful because of the motivation, conviction, and morale of their employees. Employees must care whether they do well or badly. They must believe that their efforts not only contribute to but will be recognized by the total organization.

Organizations are like individuals in that they cannot remain at a status quo. There is no permanent plateau. There is either improvement or decline. The managers of organizations and the total body of employees need to recognize this and to judge their organization's movement.

FOOTNOTES

[1] Peter F. Drucker, *The Practice of Management* (New York: Harper and Row, 1954), Chapters 10-18.

[2] Harold Koontz and Cyril O'Donnell, *Principles of Management: An Analysis of Managerial Functions*, 4th ed. (New York: McGraw Hill, 1968), p. 239.

[3] Peter F. Drucker, *Management, Tasks, Responsibilities, Practices* (New York: Harper and Row, 1973), p. 530.

[4] Koontz and O'Donnell, *Principles of Management*, Chapter 13, pp. 259-74.

[5] Henri Fayol, *General and Industrial Administration* (New York: Putnam Publishing, 1949), p. 14.

[6] *Random House Dictionary of the English Language* (New York: Random House, 1966).

[7] J. P. Mooney, *The Principles of Organization*, rev. ed. (New York: Harper and Row, 1939), Chapters 3-5, 16-18.

[8] Ibid.

[9] George S. Odiorne, "Up the Pyramid ... or ... Doughnut ... or ... Beehive," *Nation's Business* 60, no. 1 (January 1972): 62-64.

[10] Ibid., p. 63.

[11] Drucker, *Management, Tasks, Responsibilities, Practices*, pp. 532-35.

[12] Koontz and O'Donnell, *Principles of Management*, p. 423.

[13] Ernest Dale, *Planning and Developing the Company Organization Structure*, Research Report No. 20 (New York: American Management Association, 1952), pp. 138-44.

[14] Koontz and O'Donnell, *Principles of Management*, pp. 424-28.

[15] John W. Gardner, "How to Prevent Organizational Dry Rot" *Harper's Magazine* 231, No. 1385 (October 1965): 21.

[16] Ibid. Paraphrased from Gardner's article, p. 21.

4

STAFFING

Three components comprise all libraries: a physical facility or a group of facilities to house the activities of the library, a collection of resources, and personnel to collect and organize the resources and to retrieve information needed by users. Of the three components only the last—personnel—can bring a library to life and make it a dynamic, vital force for the community it serves. Most of these people—the personnel—are well educated. They are dedicated to a philosophy of service. They believe that education will improve the quality of life. And they recognize that in this age of change, a process of continuing education is essential if an individual is to be a self-sufficient, participating member of society.

LIBRARY EDUCATION

The aim here is to give no more than an historical overview of library education. However, it is important to note that the first School of Library Economy was started at Columbia College by Melvil Dewey in 1884. In 1889, the school was moved to Albany, New York, as part of the New York State Library.[1] One library school, however, was inadequate for a developing profession. In the early 1900s, many public libraries established training classes as the means of training staff. These training classes, which required a high school diploma for admission and which lasted for approximately nine months, were basically work-study programs. Students attended formal classes in the mornings and worked in the afternoons and evenings. Such subjects as cataloging, circulation, and reference were studied. Academic libraries developed in-service training programs for their potential staff.

In the 1920s and 1930s, library leaders recognized that this was an inadequate education for library professional personnel. It was recognized that the basis for library education was a broad education in the liberal arts. Strong training classes were moved from public libraries to academic institutions and the entrance requirements were raised so that a bachelor's degree was required. Basically, then, library education became a fifth year of study beyond secondary school for which a second bachelor's degree, BSLS or BALS, was awarded. There were, of course, some library education programs offered as undergraduate majors or minors as there are today. But the standard for the professional librarian until 1947 was a year of professional study beyond the baccalaureate degree, culminating in the awarding of a bachelor's degree in library science (BSLS).

In 1947, the University of Denver's Graduate School of Librarianship changed the degree offered for the fifth year of study from a BSLS to a Master of Arts. Soon other schools across the nation followed this pattern, offering various degrees (e.g., Master of Arts in Librarianship, Master of Science in Librarianship, etc.) for the fifth year of study. The present standard is that a professional librarian is an individual who holds a fifth-year master's degree from a library school accredited by the American Library Association.

The American Library Association is authorized by the Council on Postsecondary Accreditation to accredit programs leading to the first professional degree in librarianship. At the present time, over sixty programs are accredited. The *Standards of Accreditation*, 1972, as adopted by the Council of the A.L.A. in June 1972 but effective January 1, 1973, set forth the criteria for accreditation. Accreditation serves two primary purposes:

> 1) it should identify for the public including prospective students and employers educational institutions and programs of study which meet established standards of educational quality, and 2) it should stimulate improvement both in standards and in educational institutions and programs.[2]

Not all accredited programs are the same. They vary according to the goals and objectives of the individual library school. Some programs are rather prescriptive, in that they require a large group of core courses and do not permit much individualization of course selection. Others have a small core of required courses and permit students to specialize in such fields as administration, technical services, information science, and school media centers. Theoretically, at least, however, all accredited library schools should offer programs that present "the principles and procedures common to all types of libraries and library service."[3]

Employers of new graduates do not always evaluate the education that the prospective employee has received. It is assumed by employers that all accredited programs are the same. Employers should be sure that the education received by the new graduate meets the needs of the job for which the candidate is being considered.

Of course, not all personnel working in a library are required to have a master's degree and to be classified as professional librarians. Many other levels of education can be effectively utilized in libraries, ranging from a high school diploma or a baccalaureate degree, or master's degrees in subject fields or specialties such as Master of Personnel Administration, to the Ed.D or Ph.D.

In June 1970, the Council of the American Library Association adopted a statement of policy on *Library Education and Manpower*. This policy statement is given in full below because it is basic to the problem of staffing a library.

LIBRARY EDUCATION
AND PERSONNEL UTILIZATION*

A Statement of Policy Adopted by the Council of
the American Library Association, June 30, 1970**

1 The purpose of the policy statement is to recommend categories of library personnel, and levels of training and education appropriate to the preparation of personnel for these categories, which will support the highest standards of library service for all kinds of libraries and the most effective use of the variety of skills and qualifications needed to provide it.

2 Library service as here understood is concerned with knowledge and information in their several forms—their identification, selection, acquisition, preservation, organization, communication and interpretation, and with assistance in their use.

3 To meet the goals of library service, both professional and supportive staff are needed in libraries. Thus the library occupation is much broader than that segment of it which is the library profession, but the library profession has responsibility for defining the training and education required for the preparation of personnel who work in libraries at any level, supportive or professional.

4 Skills other than those of librarianship may also have an important contribution to make to the achievement of superior library service. There should be equal recognition in both the professional and supportive ranks for those individuals whose expertise contributes to the effective performance of the library.

5 A constant effort must be made to promote the most effective utilization of personnel at all levels, both professional and supportive. The tables on page 78 (Figure 1) suggest a set of categories which illustrate a means for achieving this end.

---

*The policy statement adopted by ALA with the title "Library Education and Manpower." In the spring of 1976, the Office for Library Personnel Resources Advisory Committee edited this statement to remove sexist terminology.

**Throughout this statement, wherever the term "librarianship" is used, it is meant to be read in its broadest sense as encompassing the relevant concepts of information science and documentation; wherever the term "libraries" is used, the current models of media centers, learning centers, educational resources centers, information, documentation, and referral centers are also assumed. To avoid the necessity of repeating the entire gamut of variations and expansions, the traditional library terminology is employed in its most inclusive meaning.

Figure 1

CATEGORIES OF LIBRARY PERSONNEL—PROFESSIONAL

TITLE — For positions requiring:		BASIC REQUIREMENTS	NATURE OF RESPONSIBILITY
library-related qualifications	nonlibrary-related qualifications		
Senior Librarian	Senior Specialist	In addition to relevant experience, education beyond the M.A. [i.e., a master's degree in any of its variant designations: M.A., M.L.S., M.S.L.S., M.Ed., etc.] as: post-master's degree; Ph.D.; relevant continuing education in many forms	Top-level responsibilities, including but not limited to administration; superior knowledge of some aspect of librarianship, or of other subject fields of value to the library
Librarian	Specialist	Master's degree	Professional responsibilities including those of management, which require independent judgment, interpretation of rules and procedures, analysis of library problems, and formulation of original and creative solutions for them (normally utilizing knowledge of the subject field represented by the academic degree)

CATEGORIES OF LIBRARY PERSONNEL—SUPPORTIVE

TITLE		BASIC REQUIREMENTS	NATURE OF RESPONSIBILITY
Library Associate	Associate Specialist	Bachelor's degree (with or without course work in library science); OR bachelor's degree, plus additional academic work short of the master's degree (in librarianship for the Library Associate; in other relevant subject fields for the Associate Specialist)	Supportive responsibilities at a high level, normally working within the established procedures and techniques, and with some supervision by a professional, but requiring judgment, and subject knowledge such as is represented by a full, four-year college education culminating in the bachelor's degree
Library Technical Assistant	Technical Assistant	At least two years of college-level study; OR A.A. degree, with or without Library Technical Assistant training; OR post-secondary school training in relevant skills	Tasks performed as supportive staff to Associates and higher ranks, following established rules and procedures, and including, at the top level, supervision of such tasks
Clerk		Business school or commercial courses, supplemented by in-service training or on-the-job experience	Clerical assignments as required by the individual library

6 The titles recommended here represent categories or broad classifications, within which it is assumed that there will be several levels of promotional steps. Specific job titles may be used within any category: for example, catalogers, reference librarians, children's librarians would be included in either the "Librarian" or (depending upon the level of their responsibilities and qualifications) "Senior Librarian" categories; department heads, the director of the library, and certain specialists would presumably have the additional qualifications and responsibilities which place them in the "Senior Librarian" category.

7 Where specific job titles dictated by local usage and tradition do not make clear the level of the staff member's qualification and responsibility, it is recommended that reference to the ALA category title be used parenthetically to provide the clarification desirable for communication and reciprocity. For example:

REFERENCE ASSISTANT (Librarian)   HEAD CATALOGER (Senior Librarian)

LIBRARY AIDE (Library Technical Assistant)

8 The title "Librarian" carries with it the connotation of "professional" in the sense that professional tasks are those which require a special background and education on the basis of which library needs are identified, problems are analyzed, goals are set, and original and creative solutions are formulated for them, integrating theory into practice, and planning, organizing, communicating, and administering successful programs of service to users of the library's materials and services. In defining services to users, the professional person recognizes potential users as well as current ones, and designs services which will reach all who could benefit from them.

9 The title "Librarian" therefore should be used only to designate positions in libraries which utilize the qualifications and impose the responsibilities suggested above. Positions which are primarily devoted to the routine application of established rules and techniques, however useful and essential to the effective operation of a library's ongoing services, should not carry the word "Librarian" in the job title.

10 It is recognized that every type and size of library may not need staff appointments in each of these categories. It is urged, however, that this basic scheme be introduced wherever possible to permit where needed the necessary flexibility in staffing.

11 The salaries for each category should offer a range of promotional steps sufficient to permit a career-in-rank. The top salary in any category should overlap the beginning salary in the next higher category, in order to give recognition to the value of experience and knowledge gained on the job.

12 Inadequately supported libraries or libraries too small to be able to afford professional staff should nevertheless have access to the services and supervision of a librarian. To obtain the professional guidance that they themselves cannot supply, such libraries should promote cooperative arrangements or join larger systems of cooperating libraries through which supervisory personnel can be supported. Smaller libraries which are part of such a system can often maintain the local service with building staff at the Associate level.

Figure 2

If one thinks of Career *Lattices* rather than Career *Ladders*, the flex-ibility intended by the Policy Statement may be better visualized. The movement among staff responsibilities, for example, is not necessarily directly up, but often may be lateral to increased responsibil-ities of equal importance. Each category embodies a number of promotional steps within it, as indicated by the gradation markings on each bar. The top of any category overlaps in responsibility and salary the next higher category.

Comments on the Categories

13 The *Clerk* classifications do not require formal academic training in library subjects. The assignments in these categories are based upon general clerical and secretarial proficiencies. Familiarity with basic library terminology and routines necessary to adapt clerical skills to the library's needs is best learned on the job.

14 The *Technical Assistant* categories assume certain kinds of specific "technical" skills; they are not meant simply to accommodate advanced clerks. While clerical skills might well be part of a Technical Assistant's equipment, the emphasis in an assignment should be on the special technical skill. For example, someone who is skilled in handling audiovisual equipment, or at introductory data processing, or in making

posters and other displays might well be hired in the Technical Assistant category for these skills, related to librarianship only to the extent that they are employed in a library. A *Library Technical Assistant* is a person with certain specifically library-related skills—in preliminary bibliographic searching for example, or utilization of certain mechanical equipment—the performance of whose duties seldom requires a background in general education.

15 The *Associate* categories assume a need for an educational background like that represented by a bachelor's degree from a good four-year institution of higher education in the United States. Assignments may be such that library knowledge is less important than general education, and whether the title is *Library* Associate or Associate *Specialist* depends upon the nature of the tasks and responsibilities assigned. Persons holding the B.A. degree, with or without a library science minor or practical experience in libraries, are eligible for employment in this category. Titles within the Associate category that are assigned to individuals will depend upon the relevance of their training and background to their specific assignments.

16 The Associate category also provides the opportunity for persons of promise and exceptional talent to begin library employment below the level of professional (as defined in this statement) and thus to combine employment in a library with course work at the graduate level. Where this kind of work/study arrangement is made, the combination of work and formal study should provide 1) increasing responsibility within the Associate ranks as the individual moves through the academic program, and 2) eligibility for promotion, upon completion of the master's degree, to positions of professional responsibility and attendant reclassification to the professional category.

17 The first professional category—*Librarian*, or *Specialist*—assumes responsibilities that are professional in the sense described in paragraph 8 above. A good liberal education plus graduate-level study in the field of specialization (either in librarianship or in a relevant field) are seen as the minimum preparation for the kinds of assignments implied. The title, however, is given for a position entailing professional responsibilities and not automatically upon achievement of the academic degree.

18 The *Senior* categories assume relevant professional experience as well as qualifications beyond those required for admission to the first professional ranks. Normally it is assumed that such advanced qualifications shall be held in some specialty, either in a particular aspect of librarianship or some relevant subject field. Subject specializations are as applicable in the *Senior Librarian* category as they are in the *Senior Specialist* category.

19 Administrative responsibilities entail advanced knowledge and skills comparable to those represented by any other high-level specialty, and appointment to positions in top administration should normally require the qualifications of a *Senior Librarian* with a specialization in administration. This category, however, is not limited to administrators, whose specialty is only one of several specializations of value to the library service. There are many areas of special knowledge within librarianship which are equally important and to which equal recognition in prestige and salary should be given. Highly qualified persons with specialist responsibilities in some aspect of librarianship—archives, bibliography, reference, for example—should be eligible for advanced status and financial rewards without being forced to abandon for administrative responsibilities their areas of major competence.

Implications for Formal Education

20 Until examinations are identified that are valid and reliable tests of equivalent qualifications, the academic degree (or evidence of years of academic work completed) is recommended as the single best means for determining that an applicant has the background recommended for each category.

21 In the selection of applicants for positions at any level, and for admission to library schools, attention should be paid to personal aptitudes and qualifications in addition to academic ones. The nature of the position or specialty, and particularly the degree to which it entails working with others, with the public, or with special audiences or materials should be taken into account in the evaluation of a prospective student or employee.

22 As library services change and expand, as new audiences are reached, as new media take on greater importance in the communication process, and as new approaches to the handling of materials are introduced, the kinds of preparation required of those who will be employed in libraries will become more varied. Degrees in fields other than librarianship will be needed in the Specialist categories. For many Senior Librarian positions, an advanced degree in another subject field rather than an additional degree in librarianship, may be desirable. Previous experience need not always have been in libraries to have pertinence for appointment in a library.

23 Because the principles of librarianship are applied to the materials of information and knowledge broader than any single field, and because they are related to subject matter outside of librarianship itself, responsible education in these principles should be built upon a broad rather than a narrowly specialized background education. To the extent that courses in library science are introduced in the four-year,

undergraduate program, they should be concentrated in the last two years and should not constitute a major inroad into course work in the basic disciplines: the humanities, the sciences, and the social sciences.

24 Training courses for Library Technical Assistants at the junior or community college level should be recognized as essentially terminal in intent (or as service courses rather than a formal program of education), designed for the preparation of supportive rather than professional staff. Students interested in librarianship as a career should be counselled to take the general four-year college course rather than the specific two-year program, with its inevitable loss of time and transferable content. Graduates of the two-year programs are not prohibited from taking the additional work leading to the bachelor's and master's degrees, provided they demonstrate the necessary quali- fications for admission to the senior college program, but it is an indirect and less desirable way to prepare for a professional career, and the student should be so informed.

25 Emphasis in the two-year Technical Assistant programs should be more on skills training than on general library concepts and procedures. In many cases it would be better from the standpoint of the student to pursue more broadly-based vocational courses which will teach technical skills applicable in a variety of job situations rather than those limited solely to the library setting.

26 Undergraduate instruction in library science other than training courses for Library Technical Assistants should be primarily a contri- bution to liberal education rather than an opportunity to provide technological and methodological training. This does not preclude the inclusion of course work related to the basic skills of library practice, but it does affect teaching method and approach, and implies an emphasis on the principles that underlie practice rather than how-to-do-it, vocational training.

27 Certain practical skills and procedures at all levels are best learned on the job rather than in the academic classroom. These relate typically to details of operation which may vary from institution to insitution, or to routines which require repetition and practice for their mastery. The responsibility for such in-service parts of the total preparation of both librarians and supportive staff rests with libraries and library systems rather than with the library schools.

28 The objective of the master's programs in librarianship should be to prepare librarians capable of anticipating and engineering the change and improvement required to move the profession constantly forward. The curriculum and teaching methods should be designed to serve this kind of education for the future rather than to train for the practice of the present.

29 Certain interdisciplinary concepts (information science is an example) are so intimately related to the basic concepts underlying library service that they properly become a part of the library school curriculum rather than simply an outside specialty. Where such content is introduced into the library school it should be incorporated into the entire curriculum, enriching every course where it is pertinent. The stop-gap addition of individual courses in such a specialty, not integrated into the program as a whole, is an inadequate assimilation of the intellectual contribution of the new concept to library education and thinking.

30 In recognition of the many areas of related subject matter of importance to library service, library schools should make knowledge in other fields readily available to students, either through the appointment of staff members from other disciplines or through permitting students to cross departmental, divisional, and institutional lines in reasoned programs in related fields. Intensive specializations at the graduate level, building upon strengths in the parent insitution or the community, are a logical development in professional library education.

31 Library schools should be encouraged to experiment with new teaching methods, new learning devices, different patterns of scheduling and sequence, and other means, both traditional and nontraditional, that may increase the effectiveness of the students' educational experience.

32 Research has an important role to play in the educational process as a source of new knowledge both for the field of librarianship in general and for library education in particular. In its planning, budgeting, and organizational design, the library school should recognize research, both theoretical and applied, as an imperative responsibility.

Continuing Education

33 Continuing Education is essential for all library personnel, professional and supportive, whether they remain within a position category or are preparing to move into a higher one. Continuing education opportunities include both formal and informal learning situations, and need not be limited to library subjects or the offerings of library schools.

34 The "continuing education" which leads to eligibility for Senior Librarian or Specialist positions may take any of the forms suggested directly above so long as the additional education and experience are relevant to the responsibilities of the assignment.

35 Library administrators must accept responsibility for providing support and opportunities (in the form of leaves, sabbaticals, and released time) for the continuing education of their staffs.

Additional copies available from

Office for Library Personnel Resources
American Library Association
50 E. Huron St., Chicago, Ill., 60611

Many important concepts are presented in this policy statement. Attention is called particularly to paragraphs 8 and 9, which define the role of the professional librarian. Paragraph 11 describes the basis for salary scale development, which will be discussed in detail later. Paragraphs 13 through 19 categorize the various levels of employees needed in libraries. These paragraphs amplify Figure 1 of the statement. Special attention should be given to Figure 2, which proposes two lattices (or ladders) for career movement in libraries. This concept of the professional librarian advancing up the left lattice and the specialist advancing up the right lattice is a new concept in library personnel administration. But at the present time, when the role and function of libraries are rapidly changing, it is important to utilize many people with various skills, knowledges, and abilities. The dual lattice provides for such capability.

Up to the present time, only a few libraries have implemented the concept of the two career lattices. In most libraries, the traditional pattern of one lattice still exists. The line of authority in most libraries passes down the lattice of the professional librarian. Therefore, advancement in a professional career is possible only when the employee assumes greater supervisory responsibility. There is, however, a great need for administrators to recognize the important role the specialist plays in library service and administration, and to develop organizational patterns that permit the specialist to advance in the library hierarchy because of the value of that specialty, and not simply because greater authority and responsibility are assumed.

Libraries today are identified by the U.S. Internal Revenue Service as educational institutions. The U.S. Congress, when it established the National Commission on Libraries and Information Science, approved the following policy statement (P.L. 91-345, Section 2), which enforces the federal government's recognition of the importance of libraries in a rapidly growing technological society:

The Congress hereby affirms that library and information science services adequate to meet the needs of the people of the United States are essential to achieve national goals and to utilize most effectively the Nation's educational resources and that the Federal Government will cooperate with State and local governments and public and private agencies in assuring optimum provision of such services.

The level of education achieved by members of the library staff, therefore, becomes one of the primary criteria for establishing library staffing patterns.

During the 1930s and early 1940s it was not uncommon to find libraries in which approximately 50 percent of the total staff positions were classified as professional. Following World War II and the development (at least in public institutions) of more structured personnel programs, the number of professional positions declined to approximately 30 percent of the total staff. It is anticipated that as the educational programs for professional librarians expand, the number of professional positions required in libraries may decline even more. This will occur as the professional librarian assumes more responsibility for decision-making, supervision, and training. Library Associates and other personnel as defined by the *Library Education and Manpower* policy will assume the more routine day-to-day activities.

WHAT IS A JOB?

It will be recalled that in Chapter 3, departmentation was defined as the process of identifying similar or related activities and grouping these activities into departments according to such principles as territory, function, clientele, subject, etc. The development of a job follows a similar pattern. Of the related or similar activities assigned to a department, similar or related tasks must be identified and grouped together to create a job.

Jobs should not be allowed just to emerge at the whim of the employee. And only occasionally are jobs created because of the special knowledge or ability of a particular individual. It is the responsibility of the library administration to identify the tasks that are to be included in a job. The tasks, as indicated before, should be similar or related. That is, the tasks to be accomplished by a specific job should all require approximately the same level of education. One task should not be so excessively complex that extensive education is required, while the next task is so simple that it could be performed by an individual with much less education. Further, the tasks assigned to one job should require comparable experience. Some tasks can be performed only after extensive experience in a job, while others can be executed by novices with little or no experience. And, lastly, tasks assigned to a job should require comparable responsibility. Some tasks have end responsibility. There is no review. The action of the individual in a job having end responsibility is final. Such end responsibility is frequently found in reference services, book selection, and top administration. Other jobs require little or no end responsibility. Work is reviewed. Revisers in a catalog department may have end responsibility, while the catalogers whose work is revised have no end responsibility.

It can be said, therefore, that a well-defined job has assigned to it tasks that are 1) comparable in the amount of education required, 2) comparable in the amount of experience required, and 3) comparable in the degree of responsibility required.

Other elements are also to be considered in the development of a job. That the tasks assigned a job should be similar or related has been emphasized. Tasks should be similar in that they require comparable skills, knowledges, or abilities. Skill is defined as the capability of performing manual or routine activities, operating various types of equipment, or managing an organizational unit that follows established procedures.[4] Skills are here interpreted as those activities that require less education and less experience than other jobs and that have little or no end responsibility except, perhaps, the responsibility of accuracy. Knowledges are here defined as those specific bodies of knowledge which are required in a job. The knowledge of filing rules, of the Anglo-American Cataloging Rules, of a subject field, of personnel administration, or or techniques of public relations are examples of different kinds of knowledges. The education, experience, and end responsibility required of these jobs would be higher and greater than those required for skills performance. Abilities are here defined as those activities that require the highest education and the greatest experience, and usually full end responsibility. The term refers to the capability of synthesizing a group of facts and arriving at a decision. Likewise, analyzing community needs and planning and executing programs to meet those needs is an ability. Giving a speech, conducting a meeting, appearing effectively on television is an ability. Abilities require extensive knowledge but only an understanding of skills.

Tasks should be related to the accomplishment of a single function, process, or program, or should be related to the same subject field or type of material. In larger institutions, this is easily accomplished; in small institutions, however, tasks may have to be related to more than one function, process, program, subject, or type of resource. Nevertheless, even in small institutions, the number of unrelated tasks assigned to one job should be kept as low as possible.

A job, therefore, is a planned entity consisting of assigned tasks that are similar or related in skills, knowledges, or abilities. A job, however, should not be so restrictive that assigned tasks are quickly mastered and soon become dull, monotonous, and boring. In recognition of the fact that most jobs are too small in scope, a job should be made large enough to challenge and encourage employees to grow in skills, knowledges, and abilities. There are jobs in libraries that must be performed according to prescribed procedures in order to maintain uniformity or because of standardized methodologies. These jobs are generally low in the job hierarchy of the library. Nevertheless, every opportunity should be given the employee even at this level to be creative, exercise initiative, and vary the routines as long as the established standards are maintained.

A LIBRARY PERSONNEL PROGRAM

If a library expects to make maximum utilization of its staff and at the same time to have a satisfied staff with good morale, then a clear, equitable library personnel program needs to be established. In most public institutions, school, academic and public libraries, such programs are mandated by the parent institution—the municipality or county, the state college or university, or the school district. A personnel program is designed to guarantee that all employees, regardless of race, color, creed, or sex, are treated equally and fairly.

A library personnel program consists basically of five parts: 1) the development of written job descriptions, 2) the establishment of a process to audit the actual job being performed, 3) the formation of a program to evaluate the quality of personnel performance, 4) the maintenance of a current salary scale, and 5) the development of written personnel policies. All parts of a personnel program except the results of the performance evaluation are public and should be explained thoroughly to employees. The result of the performance evaluation is privileged information available only to the employee being evaluated and those supervisors who are involved in the process or who must use the evaluations to effect personnel action. Each part will be discussed in detail.

JOB DESCRIPTIONS

The use of job descriptions to identify tasks to be performed by a specific individual or group of individuals came into wide usage during World Wars I and II. Frederick W. Taylor, of course, used job cards before this time to identify employee tasks and to prescribe the method of performing these tasks. But the concept of the job description as it is known today was somewhat expanded in World War I and to a great degree in World War II. Following World War II not only did the federal government initiate wide use of job descriptions, but state, county, and municipal governments began to require their use. Today most government agencies and many businesses and industries require job descriptions for all employees.

A job description is a written statement prepared by the administration describing the tasks that an employee is to perform, defining the relationship of the job and the employee to other units of the institution, and setting standards of education, experience, and special skills required in the job. The term "job description" is used throughout this discussion even though some authorities use the term "position description" to designate jobs in the higher echelons of an organization. Such a designation seems to reinforce the popularly held concept of the bureaucratic hierarchy, so the popular vernacular term "job description" is preferred here.

There is no standard form for a job description. Individual institutions develop the form that best meets their needs. The following outline, however, indicates what information is needed in a job description:

1) name of institution, department, and sub-department to which the job is assigned
2) date
3) job title
4) purpose and scope of the job
5) specific tasks assigned the job
6) job requirements, including institutional standards as they apply to each job.

But it is not enough to present an outline. There are specific reasons why each element is important. A discussion of each part follows.

1) Since job descriptions are used for different purposes, a clear identification of the organizational unit in which the job is located is essential.
2) Jobs change, and as a result the job description changes. Only the current job description is maintained. The date the job description was prepared indicates its currency.
3) In libraries there are no common job titles. Each library develops its own. The job title is designed to indicate the group (professional, associate, technician, or clerk) to which the job belongs and the level of the job within that grouping. Some libraries use for their professional grouping such terms as junior librarian, senior librarian, and supervising librarian. The current trend, however, is to use roman numerals to indicate levels of the professional group. The title "Librarian I" would be used to indicate the lowest level in the professional hierarchy of jobs. Librarian II and Librarian III indicate higher levels of professional jobs. If the same pattern is used to indicate levels in the clerical grouping, a Clerk I title can indicate the beginning level, while the term "Clerk II" shows that the job requires more education or experience or responsibility than the Clerk I job.
4) The statement of a job's purposes and scope includes: a) the primary responsibility of the job, b) the title of the job to whom the incumbent reports, c) the number of employees or the organizational unit supervised by this job, d) internal and external relationships required by the job.
5) The list of specific tasks assigned the job is the most important part of the job description. It identifies for the employee the exact tasks for which he will be responsible. But it also indicates to the supervisor those tasks for which training must be given, tasks that must be supervised, and tasks that must be evaluated. Without this section of the job description the whole personnel program becomes meaningless, for neither the employee nor the supervisor knows what the employee is expected to do. The tasks assigned should, of course, be comparable in education, experience, and responsibility required and should demand similar or related skills, knowledges, and abilities.
6) Job requirements are established by each individual library. Requirements that are defined include: a) amount of education required for the job, b) amount of experience required, c) special skills, knowledges, or abilities required.

Only for the beginning professional librarian is there a national standard, and that standard relates to education only. All other requirements are standards that an individual library wishes to establish. Under special skills, knowledges, and abilities the institution has the opportunity to identify capabilities needed. A bookmobile driver must be able to handle heavy equipment and must hold a special driver's license; a typist must be able to type 60 words per minute with minimal errors; a professional must be able to read and speak a foreign language. These are examples[5] of special capabilities that a library might identify as essential to a job.

Figure 4-1
Job Description for an Art Librarian in a University Library

University of _____ Library   Date

Librarian II–Art Librarian

Purpose and Scope:

To be responsible for administration and operation of the Art Library (40,000 volumes in size) and for selection, storage, retrieval, interpretation, and dissemination of the Art Library materials in support of the university's academic programs and in response to research and study needs of library patrons. This person reports to the Assistant Director for Readers' Services.

Internal relationships include regular interaction with appropriate members of the library and university staffs and with library patrons. External relationships include direct and indirect contact with university departmental representatives on campus and with other libraries and agencies off campus.

Will supervise one Library Associate and three Library Technical Assistants.

Principal Responsibilities:

Administration of the Art Library including budget preparation, planning and development of services, investigation of new equipment and techniques which can improve services and operations, training and supervision of staff, and coordination of Art Library objectives with those of the university departments, for effective fulfillment of its mission.

Selection of materials in all forms (books, periodicals, slides, microforms) for this unit in cooperation with other members of the university community, as appropriate.

Determination of records or indexes needed for maximum utilization of Art Library materials and implementing their adoption.

Interpreting Art Library collection to patrons through orientation programs, book lists, displays, exhibits, and reference, circulation, and interlibrary services.

Training and supervision of four staff members to provide effective service to patrons.

Preparation of work assignments and library schedules for this unit.

Evaluation of supervised employees.

Requirements:

Education: Master of Library Science degree, B.A. degree with Art or Art History major, reading knowledge of French. Equivalent education may be accepted.

Experience: Two years of academic library experience in reference work with some supervision and training of clerical staff or equivalent experience.

Special Skills: Understanding of library resource use requirements of Art, Art History, Architecture and related academic programs and the ability to fulfill these needs. Ability to communicate clearly in verbal and written form.

Figure 4-2
Job Description of the Director of a Public Library

_____ Public Library   Date

Director of Libraries

Purpose and Scope:

The director, under the general supervision of the library board, is responsible for the administration of the entire library system. This responsibility includes the dissemination of knowledge through the professional utilization of library resources. In cooperation with other city units the director of libraries facilitates the extension of the resources of library system to the entire legal community.

The director of libraries is expected to be in continuous control of the library system; to be able to communicate effectively with the library community, both staff and public; and to be a leader in the community while serving as the official representative of the library.

Principal Responsibilities:

1. To develop policies, services and resources to meet the immediate and long-range goals of the library and community

2. To plan, organize, implement, and evaluate the entire library's operation independently

3. To employ effective management techniques in directing, planning, organizing, staffing, coordinating, budgeting, and evaluating the library's operation

4. To analyze on a continual basis relevant influencing factors, such as the legal, physical and statistical aspects and their effect on the library's operation

5. To provide open avenues for the critical review of library operations, such as acquisitions, circulation, personnel management, and financial administration

6. To direct the administration of personnel regulations and the review of staff performance, and to approve new staff appointments, promotions and dismissals

7. To direct investigation of new trends in specific library programs and facilitate testing of new techniques, materials and equipment for improvement of the library's operational function

8. To serve as the official representative of the library system in all actions that are legally binding upon the city

9. To direct the administration of a library in-service training program, and to provide for the continuous upgrading of library personnel through the encouragement of continuing education

10. To encourage staff participation in professional socities, associations and activities at all levels

Requirements:

Education: An advanced master's degree in library science with a concentration in administration, in addition to a master's degree in library science from an ALA accredited program

Experience: A minimum of five years at the professional librarian level, with at least three years of administrative responsibility in a medium-sized or large public library

Figure 4-3
Job Description for Head of Readers' Services in a Community College

Community College   Date
Librarian III—Head of Readers' Services

Purpose and Scope:

Support the institution's instructional objectives by planning and administering Readers' Services for the students and faculty.

Works under direction of Head Librarian.

Internal relationships include continuous contact with faculty, other library staff and with library users.

External relationships include contact with professional colleagues in area to promote Readers' Services contact with publishers' representatives.

Has full supervisory responsibility over 11 people; 1 professional, 2 library associates, 3 LTA's and 5 clerks.

Principal Responsibilities:

Supervise and participate in evaluation of reference collection and the selection of materials for reference collection.

Establish and evaluate policies, practices and routines for reference, circulation and interlibrary loan.

Give reference assistance to faculty and students.

Cooperate with and involve the academic community in selection and evaluation of reference materials.

Plan and organize formal and informal library instruction for academic community.

Plan operational and capital budget for Readers' Services and recommend to Head Librarian.

Conduct in-service training for Readers' Services personnel.

Requirements:

Education: MLS and 2-3 years experience in Readers' Services.

Special Skills: managerial ability or capacity to develop it. Ability to develop knowledge of community college objectives and procedures and to relate Readers' Services program to these.

Figure 4-4
Job Description for a School Library Media Specialist*

SCHOOL LIBRARY MEDIA SPECIALIST

Title: School Library Media Specialist

Primary
Function: Plan, develop, implement, and evaluate the library/media center program of the school in line with the goals and objective of the school.

Level: Professional

Organizational
Relationships: Report and account to the District Supervisor of Library/Media Services.

Report and account to the School Principal.

Supervise media technicians, aides, clericals, adult and student volunteers.

Major
Responsibilities: Administration

Assume a leadership role within the school.

Formulate goals and objectives and identify priorities for the library/media center with the assistance and advice of the media staff, teachers, administration, and District Supervisor

Establish and implement policies that support and reinforce the goals and objectives of the school and the library/media center.

Maintain effective liaison with the District Supervisor of Library/Media Services, other supervisory and administrative staff at the district level, and the state office of the State School Library Media Specialist.

Select and supervise library/media center staff in line with established job descriptions.

Provide in-service education for teachers, students, and media center staff in the use of media and the selection and utilization of materials.

Determine and apply suitable criteria for the evaluation and selection of materials and equipment in line with stated goals and objectives.

Involve faculty and students in the evaluation of materials.

Supervise the organization, classification, processing, maintenance and circulation of the library/media center collection.

*Published by permission. Lucile Hatch, Professor, Graduate School of Librarianship, University of Denver.

Establish and supervise production services.

Provide for maintenance of materials, equipment, and facilities.

Establish access and delivery systems.

Prepare and defend the annual budgetary statement.

Evaluate the library/media program on a continuing basis, using the results to develop appropriate plans for the future.

Create, through knowledge of and skill in personnel administration, a professional atmosphere in which media staff members work harmoniously and at optimum level, and in which students and teachers can take full advantage of the resources and services of the library/media center.

Consultation

Participate in curriculum development and implementation.

Serve as instructional resources consultant and materials specialist for the various departments and the administration.

Help students acquire independence in learning and gain skill in critical thinking.

Assist students in developing competencies in listening, viewing, reading and other communication skills.

Information

Identify users' needs for information, both curricular and personal.

Develop user understanding of the strengths and limitations of the various media and equipment.

Provide instruction in the use of the library/media center and its resources.

Assist users to evaluate and select materials in reference to their needs.

Interpret content of print and nonprint materials.

Provide reference and bibliographic services.

Provide access to information available from outside agencies, people and networks.

Design media instructional packages for self instruction.

Requirements: Master's degree from an accredited library school. State certification.

Experience: None.

Length of
Contract: 10 months, including one week before school opens officially and two weeks following the official close of school.

Salary: Based on the professional salary scale for teachers (education and experience) plus three weeks salary prorated on the annual salary.

It will be noted in the above examples of job descriptions that tasks are generally defined. No standard of performance is indicated. There is an emerging trend, however, to use the job description as a means of establishing standards of performance. The quality or quantity of performance expected is stated as behavioral objectives in education are stated.

For example, it is inadequate to say, for a professional librarian, that one task is "to answer reference questions received from the public or by telephone." That task would be stated so that it could be measured: "To answer accurately reference questions received from the public or by telephone so that 80 percent of all questions received are answered to the satisfaction of the patron." The measurable factors are accuracy, quantity (80%), and patron satisfaction.

It is not difficult to measure activities that can be quantified, and many of the activities in a library can be. Even a cataloger using traditional methods might be assigned a measurable task: "To assign accurate classification and cutter numbers and appropriate subject headings and to prepare a work slip for the typists not taking more than thirty minutes for each title." Accuracy could be measured as well as output. Tauber[6] once said that no cataloger should spend more than fifteen minutes on one title, so the suggested thirty minutes is generous.

But it is very difficult to measure quality. In the example of the reference librarian, the supervisor could check accuracy by keeping a record of all questions asked and answers given. This is a time-consuming process, but perhaps it could be accomplished on a sampling basis. Patron satisfaction can also be sampled by brief questionnaires, and the 80 percent is a measurable factor. At the present time, much study is being given to the measurement of qualitative factors in librarianship. Ernest De Prospo and others are working on this type of performance measurement.[7]

The emphasis on performance emanates from the current emphasis on accountability. Librarians have performed too long without established standards against which to measure the quality and quantity of their performance. Lowell Martin[8] found, through a structured test conducted during his study of the Chicago Public Library, that many of the reference questions asked of branch librarians were inaccurately or incompletely answered. One suspects that this is not uncommon.

After all job descriptions are completed, they are arranged in a hierarchical order using required education, required experience, and the degree of end responsibility as the criteria. The job requiring the most education, experience, and responsibility will be highest in the hierarchical order and the job requiring the least of the same three criteria will be at the bottom. The jobs are being classified and a classified personnel system is created. It is the job that is being classified and not the people who will hold the job. People are never classified.

The hierarchically arranged jobs are divided into the various groupings used in the *Library Education and Manpower* policy statement. All professional positions fall in one grouping, all associate librarians in another, and library technicians, clerks, and custodians into still other groups.[9] Within each group there will be a hierarchy level based on the same three requirements given above. A job title is assigned to each level; this is where roman numerals are recommended. Jobs requiring the same level of education, experience, and responsibility are given the same title even though the tasks may be different. As shown in the examples of job descriptions, descriptive terms such as "art librarian" may be added. Figure 4-5 shows a hierarchy of professional positions.

Figure 4-5
A Hierarchy of Professional Level Jobs

Job Title	Education	Experience	End Responsibility
Librarian IV	MA from an accredited library school plus an Advanced Certificate	10 years with 3 years in supervisory positions	Final responsibility for the operation of the institution
Librarian III	MA from an accredited library school plus subject specialization	5 years professional experience	Under general supervision and according to policies, end responsibility for a department
Librarian II	MA from an accredited library school	2 years professional experience	Under general supervision and according to policies, responsible for a unit of a department
Librarian I	MA from an accredited library school	0 years of experience	Under general supervision and according to policies, performs assigned task

The same procedure for the clerical level jobs might result in a hierarchical structure as shown in Figure 4-6.

Figure 4-6
Hierarchy of Group of Clerical Level Jobs

Job Title	Education	Experience	End Responsibility
Clerk III	High school plus business school graduate	3 years experience	Under general supervision, end responsibility for payroll
Clerk II	High school plus some business school	2 years experience	Under general supervision, end responsibility for verifying invoices
Clerk I	High school diploma	0 experience	Under close supervision, perform assigned tasks

There is no standard as to how many levels may be included in each level grouping. In larger institutions there will be many; in small institutions, only a few.

However, it is very necessary that job titles be assigned to each classification level. A library might end up with a list like that illustrated in Figure 4-7.

Figure 4-7
Hierarchy of Jobs in a Classified Program

	Librarian Lattice	Specialist Lattice
Level	Librarian V	
	Librarian IV	Personnel Officer
	Librarian III	
	Librarian II	
	Librarian I	Building Engineer
	Library Associate II	
Title	Library Associate I	Library Artist
	Library Technician III	
	Library Technician II	
	Library Technician I	
	Clerk III	Key Punch Operator
	Clerk II	
	Clerk I	

This hierarchy of job titles eventually becomes the basis for the establishment of a salary scale. Each title in the Librarian Lattice indicates a different level of required education, experience, and responsibility. The specialists are placed opposite the librarian title that has comparable requirements and that would receive comparable pay.

Most job descriptions have a catch-all assignment at the end of the list of tasks. It usually reads "Other duties as assigned." The purposes of this undefined part of the job are 1) to permit flexibility in the job and 2) to provide for emergency situations. Flexibility is necessary in a job description; otherwise the individual is frozen into a set pattern of tasks. Tasks can be assigned or removed in order to allow an individual to gain new experience or to function temporarily on a different job. Any change of tasks, however, must be carefully evaluated to be sure the tasks removed or added require education, experience, and responsibility comparable to the other tasks and the general level of the job. In emergency situations, employees might be requested to perform tasks completely foreign to their regular assignments. But this type of assignment is usually temporary, lasting for a very short time.

Job descriptions as described above fulfill several important administrative and personnel needs. A job description may be used in the recruitment of new employees. Not only does the recruiter know exactly the capabilities he is searching for, but the candidate also knows exactly what would be expected of him if the job were accepted. The job description should be made available to applicants for their study and review. After an individual has been hired, the job description becomes the basis for determining training needs and identifying job tasks that will require special effort before this employee can perform them well. Later, the job description becomes the basis for formal performance evaluation.

JOB AUDIT

Employees tend to de-emphasize or ignore tasks that they don't like to perform and to expand and concentrate on tasks they like. Over a period of time an employee can change drastically the job that was originally established. It becomes necessary, therefore, to audit occasionally the jobs employees are performing to be sure that all assigned tasks are being performed.

An audit proving that all assigned tasks are being performed assures the institution that the employee is being fairly compensated. But if the audit shows that the employee has ceased doing essential tasks, the employee may be overpaid. The opposite is also true: if an employee has assumed new duties that require greater degrees of education, experience, or responsibility, then he may be underpaid. The audit will show the need for the reclassification of a job, upward or downward, and will identify jobs that need to be redefined and that thus need new job descriptions.

There are two methods of accomplishing a job audit. One method involves an interview between the employee and supervisor. The supervisor, using the job description as the basis for discussion, reviews the tasks assigned the employee. Progress achieved on each task and problems involved can be identified. The supervisor has the opportunity to recommend changes in methodology and emphasis. The supervisor must be very careful to conduct this interview in such a manner that the job audit is accomplished. This interview could become an evaluation interview, which is a completely different process conducted for a different purpose. However, the interview is not time consuming and does accomplish its purpose if the supervisor is skilled in interview techniques.

The other method of conducting a job audit is much more time consuming for both the employee and the supervisor. It requires that the employee complete a prepared form and that the supervisor analyze this information. The form usually includes the following data:

1) General information: Name of incumbent, title of position, department, name of supervisor, date, and job number (if any).
2) A list of all tasks performed by the incumbent. This list is to cover a large period of time (three or six months) and may require that some form of diary be kept by the employee. The long time period is used so that the list does not overemphasize any special assignments or emergency situations.
3) The percentage of time spent on each task: By analyzing the amount of time spent on any one task, the supervisor can determine where the employee is placing job emphasis and which tasks are being neglected or overemphasized.

After the data gathered on the job audit form have been analyzed and compared with the job description by the supervisor, an interview is still required to redirect the actions of the employee.

This method of job audit is not undertaken very frequently because of the time involved. It would certainly not be accomplished more frequently than once a year, and perhaps less often than that. The verbal job audit, the first method described, could be accomplished weekly or monthly as normal supervisory conferences are held.

If a library decided to undertake a total reclassification of all positions, a written job audit would be required. It would identify all tasks performed within the library, thus providing a list of the tasks that could be grouped together because they were similar or related. A large library would certainly have to use special personnel or a management company to accomplish total reclassification. A medium-sized or small library might use the personnel officers in municipal or county government or in academic institutions.

PERFORMANCE EVALUATION

The rating or evaluation of one person by another is as old as mankind itself. It is a natural phenomenon in the sense that individuals continually judge others by what they say, what they do, and how they affect other people. This process applies not only to work situations but to all facets of life. Such personal judgments are generally private and are not communicated to the individual.

In work situations, however, the evaluation of an employee's performance must be communicated to the individual. Without this transfer of information and the development of remedial processes or plans, the total program of evaluation is worthless. This statement is meant to establish the fact that performance evaluations conducted secretly and not communicated to the employee are not only unfair but also achieve no improvement and no redirection in performance.

Performance evaluations have important functions to fulfill in personnel program. Some of the benefits of a good performance evaluation are listed here:

1) The employee's performance is measured against job requirements as set forth in the job description.
2) The quality of performance provides a basis for personnel action such as promotion, demotion, and salary increases, and it may indicate the need for special training or retraining.
3) If properly conducted, the performance evaluation will give every level of management a better understanding of the individual's capabilities and potential within the organization.
4) The performance evaluation process should help employees establish personal goals that will enable them to grow and develop and that will further implement the institutional goals.

Each institution determines when performance evaluations will be administered. There should be a definite schedule, however, and that schedule should be public information.

In most libraries, newly appointed staff members serve a probationary period before permanent appointment is achieved. That probationary appointment may vary from one month for clerical positions or jobs in which there may be rapid turnover to one year for professional positions. A performance rating should be administered at the end of the probationary period. But a good supervisor will review with the new employee the job description and the quality of his performance during the probationary period.

After the probationary period, performance evaluations are administered on a recurring basis. Some institutions accomplish all evaluations in January of each year, or some other designated month. To place such a heavy load on supervisors usually results in poorly prepared performance evaluations. Not enough time is allowed for thoughtful, careful evaluation. Other institutions carry out performance evaluations on each anniversary of the employee's appointment to permanent status. This timetable distributes the work load over the entire year and permits careful judgments to be made.

An organization that has a program of performance evaluation must be sure that it is strongly supported by top management, because this program is basically a line function. Top management must orient and train supervisors in systematic evaluation and convince them of its value. Most supervisors dislike the process of evaluating their employees and particularly try to avoid discussing employee deficiencies with the employee. But unless top management sees that these steps are accomplished, the program will be ineffective.

One of the major problems is to establish the standards of performance against which an employee's work is judged. Standards that need to be established fall clearly into three categories:[10]

1) **Quality-quantity standards.** How well does the employee perform the various tasks set forth in the job description, and how much of each task does he accomplish?

2) **Desired effect standards.** Is work complete, accurate, and performed on time, benefiting positively the goals and objectives of the institution and users; are sound data gathered as a basis for judgments and decisions?

3) **Manner of performance standards.** Is the work accomplished in cooperation with others, without friction; can the employee adapt to new program or processes?

Because no two supervisors will interpret these standards exactly the same, top management must define the standards. This is sometimes done by issuing a performance evaluation manual. Several libraries have prepared such written documents for the supervisor's guidance. If supervisors interpret standards differently or give greater weight to one standard over another, inequity in evaluation from department to department will result. A basic criterion in any organization should be "equal pay for equal work." This can be achieved not only through the use of good job descriptions but also through comparable judgment of performance, which might result in salary increases or promotions.

There are many pitfalls in performance evaluation. Some of the most common errors are described in the Denver Public Library's *Manual for Performance Evaluation*[11]

1) **The error of the "halo effect":** Supervisors often evaluate the employee in terms of their personal mental attitude about the employee rather than by careful attention to the individual factors of work performance. He may be a "nice person", but still do poor work. (The opposite of the "halo effect"—down-grading someone you dislike but whose work is good—is also an error.)

2) **The error of "prejudice and partiality":** Not only is it an error of judgment but also a Constitutional violation to consider race, creed, color, religion, politics, nationality and sex in evaluating work performance.

3) **The error of "leniency, softness, or spinelessness":** This is the most common error—taking the easy way out. It occurs when supervisors can't face the unpleasantness that might arise from an unfavorable evaluation. "Spineless" ratings tag a supervisor as weak and therefore unfair to his really good employees. Effects of this error force ratings so drastically to the top of the scale that they are valueless to us and others in management. Such an error also creates an unrealistic feeling of success when improvement in performance is badly needed and often possible. Many supervisors believe that their bosses think that low ratings reflect poor supervision; thus, standard or above ratings may become defenses for the supervisor. He may presume that some supervisors do not rate honestly and that he must upgrade ratings to avoid penalizing his employees.

4) **The error of the "central tendency"**: On a normal distribution curve more people will be rated closer to the mean than to any other point on the scale. A rating which is near the norm becomes a central tendency error if it does not reflect true performance. It is most likely to occur when a supervisor is careless or lazy about the rating or does not know the worker well.

A standard rating for unusually good or poor performance is unfair—to the employee, his fellow workers and the Denver Public Library.

5) **The error of "contrast"**: Is this rating a measure of the work that this employee has actually accomplished or is it a measure of what I think he has the potential to do?

6) **The error of "association"**: In the process of rating, busy raters will sometimes rate factors at the same degree merely because they follow each other on the page. This may also happen when the supervisor is tired, or bored, and tries to make hurried judgments without all the facts.

There are no standard performance evaluation forms. Each institution usually prepares its own forms to meet its own requirements. Frequently staff committees are asked to develop the form by which they wish their work to be evaluated. In larger libraries, the personnel office is sometimes responsible for devising a form.

The first job of any group building a performance evaluation form is to determine the traits, characteristics, abilities, and skills on which they will be judged. The listing of all possible elements may indicate the desirability of having two forms—one for professionals and one for other classifications. But most institutions develop only one form, which lists all desirable elements but which provides a method to indicate those elements not appropriate to a particular job. Some elements that usually appear on evaluation forms are quality of work, quantity of work, job knowledge, cooperation, initiative, self-reliance, ability to get along with others, dependability, leadership, and appearance. Sometimes these broad elements are broken down into sub-elements. Dependability could be subdivided into 1) discharge of own job responsibilities, 2) regular and punctual attendance, and 3) self-control. Perhaps it is an understatement to say that it is easy to reach consensus on the basic elements to be included in the evaluation form. But consensus must eventually be reached.

The more difficult part of building an evaluation form concerns the manner in which the individual's performance of each element is indicated. Many forms use a horizontal line after each element with degrees of success indicated, as shown below:

Initiative: The ability to develop new pattern of activity.

Poor   Fair   Average   Good   Excellent

The element being judged is given first, followed by a statement clarifying what is meant by that element. The horizontal line below the statement has words above it that describe varying degrees of success. The supervisor indicates the evaluation of the employee for that element by placing a check or X at the appropriate place on the horizontal line. But can any two people agree as to the meaning of average, or fair, or excellent? No matter how much training a supervisor is given, these terms will be interpreted differently to the detriment of employees. Nevertheless, many institutions, libraries and others, use forms based on this pattern.

In recent years the inadequacy of this form has been recognized. A new pattern has developed which eliminates such words as poor, average, good. A short phrase is used to describe different levels of performance. The most difficult part is to develop a short phrase that cannot be misinterpreted, thus assuring comparable interpretation by various supervisors of the elements included on the performance evaluation. If *accuracy* were the element being evaluated, such phrases as the following might be used to show various degrees of accuracy.

Exceptionally accurate; rarely makes errors

Fairly accurate; infrequent errors

Moderately accurate; acceptable number of errors

Below minimum requirements; frequent errors

It does not make any difference how many levels of an element are defined. Generally four or five are given. In the example above, four levels of accuracy are defined. The following evaluation form is the product of a staff Committee of the Denver Public Library[12], which developed a performance evaluation form clearly showing the employee his strengths and weaknesses. Also, the form is designed to record results of the performance evaluation interview and to indicate the future goals agreed on by employee and supervisor.

This method of defining the level of performance for each element used on a performance evaluation form is being adopted by many libraries. The rater and the employee both understand better the evaluation that has been given. There is little possibility of misinterpretation.

It will be noticed that the evaluation form shown in Figure 4-8 has space for the supervisor's comments. These comments, relating to each of the elements being evaluated, are desirable. However, the form ought to provide space for the supervisor to record the results of the performance evaluation interview, which will be discussed later. Also, space must be provided for the supervisor's signature, the signature of the employee, and the date of the interview.

The process of administering a performance evaluation program is not difficult.

1) An office is responsible for distributing to supervisors the evaluation forms according to the determined schedule. The office that has this responsibility varies according to the size of the organization. A

Figure 4-8
Performance Evaluation Form, Denver Public Library*

DENVER PUBLIC LIBRARY

PERFORMANCE EVALUATION

Type: Annual _____   Name _____

     Midpoint _____   Job

     Probation _____   Classification _____

     Completion _____   Branch or

     Probation _____   Department _____

                     Rating

     Terminal _____   Period   From: _____ To: _____

                     THIS EVALUATION MUST BE COMPLETED AND

     Transfer _____   RETURNED TO THE PERSONNEL OFFICE BY: _____

CIRCLE DEGREE APPLICABLE FOR EACH FACTOR

                                                        ADDITIONAL COMMENTS

Factor			
1. ACCURACY OF WORK	a. Exceptionally accurate	c. Work usually acceptable	
	b. Maintains high standards	d. Below minimum requirements	
2. THOROUGHNESS IN HANDLING DETAILS	a. Exceptionally thorough	c. Moderately careful	
	b. Usually thorough	d. Work frequently incomplete	
3. QUANTITY OF WORK	a. Accomplishes high volume of work	c. Quantity usually acceptable	
	b. Quantity acceptable	d. Quantity low, unacceptable	
4. OUTPUT UNDER STRESS	a. Highly dependable under pressure	c. Sometimes inadequate under pressure	
	b. Usually dependable under pressure	d. Inadequate under pressure	
5. TIME SPENT PRODUCTIVELY	a. Makes best use of time	c. Sometimes ineffective	
	b. Keeps busy effectively	d. Wastes time	
6. KNOWLEDGE OF OWN JOB	a. Exceptional knowledge	c. Basic knowledge	
	b. Considerable knowledge	d. Limited - often inadequate knowledge	
7. KNOWLEDGE OF DPL GOALS AND POLICIES	a. Highly knowledgeable	c. Basic knowledge	
	b. Better than usual knowledge	d. No interest beyond own job	
8. COURTESY AND HELPFULNESS WITH PATRONS	a. Enthusiastic and courteous	c. Does not offer but helps on request	
	b. Easily approached, responsive	d. Indifferent	
9. RELATIONS WITH FELLOW WORKERS	a. Extremely well liked	c. Accepted	
	b. Well liked	d. Induces antagonisms	

*Reproduced with permission.

10. HOUSEKEEPING, WORK AREA, ETC.	a. Conscientiously maintains neatness of surroundings	c. Indifferent about appearance of work area	
	b. Keeps own area neat, orderly	d. Uncooperative in housekeeping details	
11. SELF-IMPROVEMENT (Eagerness to advance within D. P. L.)	a. Systematically prepares for more advanced work	c. Limited ambition; little effort to improve	
	b. Puts forth effort to improve and learn	d. Displays no ambition or desire to progress	
12. APPEARANCE	a. Always clean, neat and appropriately dressed	c. Sometimes untidy	
	b. Usually neat, clean and suitably dressed	d. Poor appearance is usual	
13. VITALITY, ENERGY	a. Abundant energy well directed	c. Fair health; work not adversely affected	
	b. Strong endurance; rarely ill	d. Lacks stamina; cannot give required effort	
14. LEARNING ABILITY	a. Excellent comprehension and retention	c. Must be reinstructed often	
	b. Seldom needs reinstruction	d. Poor; reinstruction ineffective	

ADDITIONAL COMMENTS

15. ADAPTABILITY (Ability to accept new ideas and situations)	a. Exceptionally eager to try new ideas	c. Slow to change from old ideas and procedures	
	b. Receptive to change and new ideas	d. Will not accept new methods or change	
16. ATTITUDE TOWARD CRITICISM	a. Uses and profits by criticism	c. Sometimes resents criticism	
	b. Acts upon criticism	d. Resists criticism	
17. DECISION MAKING	a. Assembles facts and makes sound decisions	c. Indecisive	
	b. Usually makes reliable decisions	d. Unreliable	
18. RESOURCEFULNESS (Ingenuity)	a. Highly creative; comes up with new and useful ideas	c. Able to develop ideas on routine matters	
	b. Has imagination; usually a source of usable ideas	d. Rarely has a usable idea	
19. REGULARITY IN ATTENDANCE	a. Rarely absent	c. Irregular attendance	
	b. Absences within acceptable limits	d. Excessive absence	
20. PUNCTUALITY (On duty promptly; keeps appointments)	a. Ready for duty promptly	c. Careless about punctuality	
	b. Usually punctual	d. Excessive tardiness	
21. POISE AND SELF-CONTROL	a. Self-controlled in any situation	c. Tends to lose control	
	b. Usually self-controlled	d. Easily upset	
22. DISPOSITION (Temperament)	a. Consistently cheerful	c. Uneven disposition	
	b. Pleasant under most circumstances	d. Seldom pleasant	
23. LEADERSHIP	a. Motivates others exceptionally well	c. Does not always get good results	
	b. Gets good results from others	d. Ineffective as a leader	
24. ORGANIZATION OF WORK	a. Analyzes and organizes work thoroughly	c. Work sometimes lacks proper planning	
	b. Organizes work satisfactorily	d. No ability to organize work	
25. SKILL IN TRAINING	a. Develops staff to high degree of efficiency	c. Sometimes fails to instruct well	
	b. Achieves progress with most staff members	d. No training ability	
26. EVALUATING PERSONNEL	a. Accurately evaluates abilities and character	c. Evaluations too often inaccurate	
	b. Evaluations usually accurate and objective	d. Poor evaluations; lacks insight	

27. PROFESSIONAL INTERESTS AND ACTIVITIES	a. Keen interest and active participation	c. Moderate interest, but little participation	
	b. Interested, but participation limited	d. No interest or participation	
28. APPLICATION OF PROFESSIONAL KNOWLEDGE	a. Consistent; appropriate; skillful	c. Limited effectiveness	
	b. Usually effective	d. Ineffective	
29. AWARENESS OF COMMUNITY	a. Accurately evaluates community needs and interests	c. Considers only obvious community needs	
	b. Interested in service to community	d. Lacks interest in community needs	

SUMMARY OF PERFORMANCE EVALUATION: Supervisors are to list in the space below factors which are rated "C" or "D" or which need improvement. Indicate action being undertaken by supervisor and staff member to improve the factor concerned, and when that action is to be completed.

FACTOR (Name)	RATING	ACTION AGREED UPON	DATE TO BE COMPLETED

In what areas of the job assignment and in what traits does this staff member excel? _____

Has this staff member any special abilities or skills not being used on present job? _____

Do you have any definite recommendations, such as: placing or taking off probation; transfer; termination; merit increase; evaluation of the job itself; etc.?

_____

_____

_____

Rater's
Signature: _____

My Supervisor reviewed this evaluation with me on (date) _____

Rater's
Title: _____

Signature of
Staff Member: _____

Date of
Discussion: _____

Signature of
Reviewing Rater: _____

Date
Reviewed: _____

DPL 654 4/71

personnel office, the librarian's office, or an administration assistant might be responsible. That office is responsible for identifying the individual whose performance is to be evaluated, the department in which the job is located, the name of the supervisor responsible for completing the form, and the date the form is due back in the initiating office.

2) The supervisor receiving the form now becomes the rater. The rater is the employee's immediate supervisor, who supposedly knows the most about the job being evaluated. It is the rater's responsibility to complete the form thoughtfully and carefully. Sometimes it is wise for the rater to base judgments on written notes or a diary kept over a period of time. The rater must have proof of evaluations given—particularly negative evaluations. Also, the rater should consider the employee's work from the last period of rating to the current time; evaluation should not be based on what happened last week or last month. But the rater must not be afraid to give negative ratings. Libraries have for too long a time been willing to tolerate incompetent employees. With today's emphasis on accountability and in view of the economic condition of most libraries, it is the rater's absolute responsibility to be accurate and truthful in the evaluation of an employee's performance. It not infrequently happens that a rater rates an employee as adequate or good only to request the employee's discharge or transfer a few months later. If the employee is bad, say so, but have proof; if the employee is good, mark the evaluation form accordingly.

3) Sometimes the rater is conscientiously or unconscientiously prejudiced against an employee. Prejudice arises not only from race or creed but occasionally from such facts as color of hair, personality, physical characteristics, etc. In order to make sure that no prejudice or bias influences an evaluation rating, the rating should be reviewed by the supervisor's supervisor—the next person in the hierarchy. Together the rater and the next supervisor should review the proposed performance evaluation and come to a consensus on the accuracy of the evaluation.

4) Conducting the performance evaluation interview is probably the most difficult part of the process. At least it is the part most dreaded by employees and supervisors. Very specific steps should be taken to prepare for this interview. A specific appointment should be established with the employee by the supervisor, and the purpose of the appointment should be made clear. Before the meeting is held, the employee should receive the accomplished performance evaluation form. The employee should have at least 24 hours to review the evaluation of his work and to consider its fairness and appropriateness. The supervisor also has to prepare for the meeting. Previous performance evaluations might be examined to review the employee's progress. Certainly the supervisor must plan how the meeting is to be structured. The accomplishment of these two steps eliminates two of the most

prevalent errors in performance evaluation interviews, since 1) the employee has time to study the evaluation instead of being suddenly handed an evaluation without time to think about it; 2) the supervisor plans the meeting instead of calling it on sudden impulse in an attempt to get it out of the way rapidly.

Because of the sensitivity of this interview, it is necessary for the supervisor to establish as informal and permissive an atmosphere as possible. Frequently supervisors eliminate the barrier and symbol of their authority by moving from their desk to an area having lounge furniture. Many supervisors do not realize the psychological obstacle a desk creates. Techniques of a good interview dictate that the supervisor ask questions or make comments that will encourage the employee to talk. The supervisor should not lecture the employee. If the employee is encouraged to talk, the discussion will naturally center on the performance evaluation. The employee has the opportunity to express concern or approval of the evaluation, the supervisor can explain why certain elements were rated as they were but should always lead back to the employee. Listed below are objectives that the supervisor hopes to accomplish through this interview:

1)   to identify problems the employee has in performing any assigned tasks;
2)   to plan methods or procedures by which these problems might be resolved;
3)   to determine the employee's general level of satisfaction with the job, the institution, and the working environment;
4)   to help the employee plan future personal programs and activities that will make him more effective in the job or that will help him prepare for advancement.

The last objective given above is particularly important. Together the employee and the supervisor are establishing current and long-range goals for the employee. Such goals (progress and objectives), after mutual agreement, are recorded on the performance evaluation form, and at the next evaluation interview progress toward these goals is measured. By signing the performance evaluation form, the employee indicates acceptance of the evaluation and proposed goals.

Of course, not all interviews will go as smoothly as indicated above. In some cases the supervisor may have to take such action as demoting or terminating an employee. But the supervisor should be able to anticipate when such action might be necessary and to be prepared for these situations. Previous evaluations and the current performance evaluation would provide one indication, and the known attitude and behavior of the employee would provide other signals that difficulty might be encountered. The smart supervisor is the one who is seldom caught unprepared for any direction the interview takes.

Performance evaluation is a necessary but difficult part of personnel administration. The rationale for it is that if employees are told where their performance is deficient, they will take steps to correct such deficiencies. But, as Gellerman points out, this is an oversimplification. He says that "it would be more accurate to say that most men would want to correct the deficiencies in their performance if they *agreed* that they were deficient and if there appeared to be enough *advantage* in correcting them to justify the effort."[13] The dichotomy of these two philosophies is the reason why performance evaluation frequently results in resentment and tension between the supervisor and the employee.

Granted, performance evaluation may be an imperfect tool in personnel administration. Nevertheless, it can be made more effective if, as stated earlier, the program is strongly supported by top management. If it is viewed as a tool of second- or third-level supervisors it loses its clout. Then it encourages strife. But if it is given strong top support and if it uses objective standards for evaluation, it helps the employee to understand where he stands—and that is something all employees want to know.

SALARY ADMINISTRATION

The largest expenditure of most libraries is for employee salaries. Even though some libraries try to differentiate between "wages" for certain lower-level or hourly employees and "salaries" for upper echelon personnel, it is all money spent to compensate the people who make the library function. Since libraries, as compared to businesses and industries, do not operate for profit and therefore cannot offer annual bonuses, stock options, or other special forms of remuneration, salaries, which includes fringe benefits, become the only method of compensating employees for their labor.

Most libraries receive their total salary fund from the institution to which they are attached. For public libraries, is the municipality, the county, or other political structures. Academic libraries receive their funds from the parent educational institution, as do school media centers. A few libraries receive personnel funds from endowments, from federal or foundation grants, or, to a minor degree, from earned income. Funds received from federal or foundation grants are allocated for specific projects or programs on a one-time or temporary basis, and such funds are considered "soft" money as compared to funds for permanently authorized positions.

Private businesses and institutions are not required to make public the salaries paid any individual or group of employees. Indeed, in most industries salary information is a closely kept secret. Public institutions, on the other hand, are required to make salary information available to anyone. Some employees are not concerned that their salary is public information; others are concerned for they believe the amount of money they earn is indicative of their worth as an individual. Jealousies and insidious comparisons sometimes result from public disclosure of salary information.

In libraries, a salary administration program consists of three parts: 1) the determination of what salary to pay, 2) the development of a salary scale, and 3) the process of awarding salary increases.

Determination of Salary to be Paid

All institutions that pay personnel for services rendered must determine what is a fair and equitable compensation for the education, experience, and responsibility required in the job. It can be assumed that a job requiring more of each of these three criteria would receive more pay than a job that requires less. But that assumption is not necessarily true today because of the power of labor unions. Some professions in which a high degree of education is required receive less compensation than labor groups who have good manual skills and lower educational requirements. Perhaps this accounts for the present decline in college and university undergraduate enrollment.

Institutions that wish to recruit and retain highly qualified personnel must offer salaries that are competitive in the job market. Individuals who have specialized education, who have demonstrated capability resulting from successful work experience, and who are willing to accept responsibility are always in demand. But the compensation must be adequate to attract them to a job. While money may not be the major motivator for some people, it is still very important to most. Institutions that hope to obtain the best people and to retain their services will offer salaries higher than institutions that will accept less performance and anticipate turnover.

While it is generally considered that the salaries of professional librarians are competitive nationally, there are regional and local conditions which affect salaries. In large metropolitan centers such as the New York area, the cost of living is greater than in smaller communities. Factors of this nature will affect the level of salaries offered. The annual report of professional salaries received by current graduates of accredited library schools, usually published in the July issue of *Library Journal*,[14] shows the regional variation of beginning salaries as well as the national average and median salaries. It must be emphasized that this information is for the beginning or entry position into the field of librarianship.

In reality, the entry position is the only position for which the job requirements can be accurately described. While there are some exceptions, the entry position usually requires 1) five years of education beyond the secondary school with the fifth year culminating in graduation from an accredited library school, 2) no professional experience, and 3) minimal or moderate end responsibility in job performance. The requirements of other levels of professional positions will vary from institution to institution. Thus, many institutions use this entry level salary as the basis for their salary scale.

There are several ways to gather information on entry level salaries as well as on other professional level jobs. The annual article in the *Library Journal* has already been mentioned. But an institution may wish to gather this data by using a salary survey, or simply by evaluating salaries offered in advertisements in professional periodicals. Some state libraries issue salary data for all libraries of the state. Regardless of the method used, great care must be taken to assure that the data gathered are for positions that have the same job requirements.

If it is decided to conduct a salary survey to gather salary data, the following standards for the survey must be followed:

1) The libraries selected to be surveyed must be comparable in size.
2) The libraries must be located in communities or institutions with comparable population or enrollment.
3) The libraries selected must represent a geographic distribution covering the United States.
4) The job level for which salary information is being solicited must be clearly defined. As mentioned above, the entry level professional position is the only professional position that is comparable. However, other special positions, such as a personnel officer, can be described adequately to acquire comparable information.

When the data are received from libraries participating in the survey, the salaries are placed in rank order, with the highest at the top and lowest at the bottom. Taking into consideration such factors as competition in the job market, quality of personnel desired, and the ability of the local institution or political unit to pay, a decision must be reached concerning the salary figure to be accepted. The median of salaries identified through the survey might be accepted, or the average, or the average of the highest quartile, or the median of the lowest quartile. It is up to the governing body or institutional officials to make the decision. But a decision must be made. That figure then becomes the dollar value assigned to the position or positions surveyed.

The one danger of basing salaries on a survey is the fact that the survey reports salaries that are currently being paid, while the library making the survey is planning to use the figures for future salaries. The salaries of the surveying library, therefore, will be at least a year behind salaries being paid by those libraries included in the survey.

Salaries for library positions other than the professional grouping are usually determined by the going rate of pay in the community in which the library is located. Of course, careful attention has to be given to the requirements of each job to be sure the employee receives adequate compensation for the education, experience, and responsibility required by the job. Information concerning local salaries can be obtained from such agencies and institutions as the school system, local government, employment agencies, and sometimes Chambers of Commerce. If desired, a library can conduct a salary survey within a community. The standards for a survey given above should be carefully observed.

Development of a Salary Scale

Only a few years ago it was not unusual for an employer to set a single dollar amount for job compensation. If that amount was changed, it was at the whim of the employer. As a result, unequal pay was given for comparable work. In many cases, employees were unfairly treated as adjustments in pay depended on the employer's attitude and feeling toward that employee. This practice still exists today, particularly in small or medium-sized businesses that are owner operated.

But large industries, businesses, governmental agencies, and public institutions have been forced by employee and union pressure to develop more efficient and objective methods of salary administration. One method involves the establishment of specific salary scales for each job classification used in the organization. How classifications are established in libraries was discussed above, under the heading "Job Descriptions." Figure 4-6 above shows a hierarchy of jobs which might be used in a library.

A salary scale establishes the amount of money that will be paid for the accomplishment of duties designated in the job description. The scale has a minimum and a maximum amount that will be paid for that job. The minimum represents the beginning or entry level salary and the maximum amount indicates the value of the job to the institution when it is performed with maximum efficiency and thoroughness. The difference between the minimum and the maximum is known as the salary range for that job. In between the minimum and the maximum are steps on the salary scale, which designate salary increases awarded the employee as proficiency increases or as experience is gained. There is no standard for the number of steps to be included on a salary scale. It is common to find salary scales with six to eight steps, but some have as many as twelve. The dollar increase from one step to another depends on the institution—there is no standard. Generally, however, the difference from one step to the next ranges from 3 percent to 5 percent of the total salary. The more steps there are on a salary scale the smaller the percentage increase between steps. Once the percentage between steps is determined, it should be applied equally to all scales. Employers sometimes use a larger percentage between steps for salaries of the lower paying jobs and a smaller percentage increase for higher paying jobs. Such a practice results in a compression of the salary scale and is unfair to employees in higher salary brackets.

Some administrators and employers believe that salary schedules should not overlap. Figure 4-9 shows the relationship of non-overlapping salary scales. For each level of the clerk grouping, the minimum and maximum of the salary range is represented by the top and bottom of the vertical rectangles, and salary scale steps are shown between these parameters.

Figure 4-9
Relationship of Salaries in a Non-Overlapping Scale

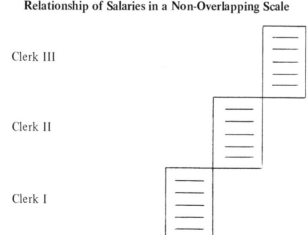

It is a more common practice, however, to have overlapping salary scales. Usually the last one-third of the first scale forms the first one-third of the next scale. The overlap philosophy is dictated by the assumption that an experienced, efficient employee in a lower classed job is more valuable to the institution than an inexperienced employee in a job with a higher classification. For the professional grouping shown in Figure 4-5 (page 96) an overlapping salary scale would have the following relationship.

Figure 4-10
Relationship of Salaries in an Overlapping Scale

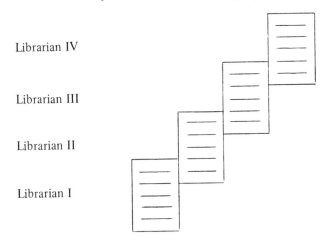

A salary scale of six steps each for Librarian I and Librarian II jobs is shown in Figure 4-11. A 5 percent increment is used, but figures are rounded out to the nearest dollar value. Salary figures are illustrative and in no way constitute a recommendation for entry level salaries. The salary figures used represent monthly salaries. On a salary scale either monthly or annual salaries may be used.

Figure 4-11
Salary Scale

Step	A	B	C	D	E	F
Job Title						
Librarian II	1042*	1094	1149	1206	1266	1270
Librarian I	900*	945	992	1042	1094	1149

*Indicates entry level salary.

The same process carried out for all levels of the professional grouping shown in Figure 4-7 (page 97) would complete the salary scale for a library having five levels of professional jobs. But the salary scale, once established, is not a fixed and permanent personnel tool. Rather, it is a scale that has to be changed at least annually. As long as inflationary trends dominate the American economy, it can be anticipated that the findings of wage surveys will cause salary scales to increase. There may come a time, however, when they decrease. Regardless of the way they move, the principle of establishing a salary scale remains the same.

There are three principles that should be observed when administering a salary scale:

1) Not all employees are required to enter a salary scale at the first step. If it is the policy of the institution to recognize previous related work experience, a new employee might enter higher on the scale. The principle is that new employees should enter the scale at the same step as other employees who have comparable education, experience, and responsibility.

2) On Figure 4-11, if a Librarian I who at Step D of the salary scale and who is receiving $1042 per month is promoted to Librarian II, that employee should not be forced to take a salary cut because of the promotion. The principle is that an employee when promoted to a higher position should receive a salary increase. By this principle the promoted employee would receive $1094. Some libraries have policies that permit the promotion but not the salary increase, but such policies are unfair because the employee is assuming more responsibility and should be so compensated.

3) If a new salary scale is adopted by the institution, the employee who has moved up the scale should remain at the same step. The principle is that if an employee because of quality service or length of service has advanced up the scale, he remains at the same step even if the scale changes, since otherwise his previous reward for meritorious or continuous service is withdrawn.

Awarding Salary Increases

Two philosophies dictate the basis for awarding salary increases. One philosophy holds that an employee is entitled to a salary increase because of continual service. The salary adjustment becomes automatic and is usually awarded on the anniversary of the employee's appointment. This philosophy is based on the assumption that continuous service means improved work. That assumption has not been proven true. Sometimes service over a long period of time permits the development of poor work habits and declining efficiency. Also, the employee's knowledge that a salary increase will be forthcoming if he maintains minimal performance creates a negative attitude toward the job. Despite this, many organizations operate their salary program on an automatic annual plan.

The other philosophy is based on the concept that salary increases should be awarded only for quality performance. It is assumed that awards in the form of a larger salary encourage employees to perform more efficient work. This assumption may be based on the findings of social scientists that money is a strong motivator. Money is a motivator at least for a period of time. If an organization follows this philosophy, only a part of the work force will receive salary adjustments. No award is made to those employees whose work is below standard.

Regardless of the philosophy that dictates an organization's salary program, some form of performance evaluation is needed. The function of the performance evaluation procedure in organizations giving automatic salary increases is to encourage the employee to set personal goals that will correct poor work habits and increase the quality of work. The employee knows that average performance will result in increased pay. The possibility that the supervisor can motivate the employee to do better work is reduced. The employee knows that average performance will result in increased pay. The possibility that the supervisor can motivate the employee to do better work is reduced. But when merit, as determined by the performance evaluation, becomes the basis for salary increases, the employee is much more concerned with work performance. The evaluation is important and the resulting awards for good work are gratifying. The supervisor has a greater possibility of guiding the employee into good work habits and the production of good work.

Whether the salary program is based on service or on merit, nothing in a salary program limits the employee's movement on the salary scale to only one step at a time. For outstanding service and major contributions to an organization, an employee might be moved two or more steps on the salary scale at one time.

FRINGE BENEFITS

Most businesses and industries, including libraries, pay for a group of supplementary items called fringe benefits. The cost of fringe benefits is an additional cost to the organization, and most employees do not recognize that fringe benefits are a supplement to their salary.

Exactly which fringe benefits will be offered employees is generally determined by the organization's management. There are, however, a few that are required by law. Federal and state laws as well as labor contracts resulting from collective bargaining establish certain fringe benefits.

The Social Security Act of 1935, as amended, requires that employers collect through salary deduction a percentage of the employee's salary up to a designated amount. That sum, matched by a like sum paid by the employer, is paid to the federal government on a quarterly basis. In recent years both the percentage withheld from the employee and then matched by the employer and the salary amount on which the tax is imposed have continued to rise.

The Federal Unemployment Tax Act of 1935, as amended, requires employers of four or more employees covered by the Act to pay a percentage of the employees' salaries to the federal government to cover unemployment insurance.

Workman's Compensation, established by state laws, provides for payment to employees for injuries or diseases received or contracted as the result of job-oriented accidents or working conditions. Medical care, rehabilitation services, and death benefits are included. The employer bears the total cost of this program, though there are different methods from state to state of maintaining insurance programs to cover this cost.

State and federal programs cover more than 85 percent of salaried employees in the United States.[15] Hourly workers in small companies or workers doing domestic work are sometimes not covered. Also, some institutions maintain a separate retirement program and are not part of Social Security.

The Equal Pay Act has also had a strong impact on fringe benefits. This Act provides that it is "an unlawful employment practice for an employer to discriminate between men and women with regard to fringes."[16] This provision challenges programs that have different retirement requirements for men and women, different rules for the "head of the household" or "principal wage earner." Also under this Act, maternity leaves must be treated as temporary leave comparable to disability due to injury, surgery, or other incapacity.

In addition to the fringe benefits mandated by federal or state laws, institutions and organizations establish other forms of employee benefits. For some, the employer pays the full cost, while for others there is a shared payment. These can be grouped into four categories:

1) Supplementary health and insurance programs. Special group life insurance programs are frequently available, as are health and hospital programs. In some recent labor negotiations, dental insurance has been proposed.
2) Paid rest periods and lunch breaks.
3) Payment for time not worked includes vacations, sick leave, holidays, and leave because of State or National Guard duty, jury duty, death in the family, and personal business.
4) Other fringe benefits include special programs such as employee credit unions, service and suggestion awards, travel and moving expenses, and educational tuition refunds.

Most of the fringe benefits listed above are available in libraries—at least, in larger libraries. Employees tend to take fringe benefits for granted. They do not realize that fringe benefits are a significant part of the total labor cost of a library. Nor do they realize that fringe benefits add to their salary because of the contribution to these programs made by the employer. There are no studies of the cost of fringe benefit programs to libraries. Indeed, there is little information concerning fringe benefits in industry as a whole. Generally, when wage surveys are made no exploration of fringe benefit programs is conducted. Therefore, the dollar value of the fringe benefit program of any one institution cannot be compared to that of another. On a percentage basis, however, the cost of such programs in recent years has been increasing substantially and more rapidly than basic salaries.

In 1972, the Chamber of Commerce of the United States made a study of employee benefits.[17] This study found that in 1952 the cost of fringe benefits was 20.7 percent of the total payroll and that by 1971 that cost had risen to 34.5

percent. However, because of the wide variation in fringe benefit programs, the study cited above indicated that the cost varies from 14 percent to more than 50 percent of total payroll.[18]

Employees no longer view the library's fringe benefit program as a privilege, but rather as a right. It is believed that the years ahead will see an increase in such programs. Therefore, a library manager contemplating the establishment of a fringe benefit must carefully study the program to determine the future financial impact of the program on the institution. But even more important, after determining that the program is needed and desired by the employees, he must carefully define the program establishing such policies, procedures, and rules as necessary to assure its fair and equitable implementation.

PERSONNEL POLICIES, PROCEDURES AND RULES

As institutions grow, a body of policies, procedures, and rules develops. It was mentioned in Chapter 2 that as an organization is structured, organizational policies are written so that organizational continuity is maintained. Likewise, as personnel programs are established, personnel policies, procedures and rules are written 1) to guarantee program consistency, 2) to assure equitable and comparable interpretation of the program, and 3) to maximize the equal and fair application of the program to all employees.

A policy is defined as a statement that establishes a definite course or method of action to guide and determine present and future decisions. In no sense are policies engraved in stone and unchangeable. But they usually have a high degree of permanence.

Within the framework of the definition given above, it should be recognized that a policy is a broad statement of intent. The policy establishes guidelines for subordinate decision makers; it keeps all units of the organization moving in the same direction.

The preparation of policy statements can encourage participative management. Seldom does one person assume responsibility for policy determination. Rather, a group of supervisors or staff members might recommend the establishment or modification of a policy. Discussing, evaluating, and writing the policy statement can encourage the participation of those groups who will be affected by it.

Particularly in the field of personnel administration, clearly defined policies are needed. The employees of a library need to understand, through written policy statements, what the classified personnel program is, how it operates, why salaries are administered in a particular way, why and what the performance evaluation is, what fringe benefits are available, and all other factors that affect them personally.

A procedure is defined as a series of specific actions or operations that lead to a desired end. A procedural statement sets forth the steps essential for accomplishing a particular result. While there may be many statements of procedure throughout a library, there are not many in personnel administration. Only in programs that require comparable action are procedures necessary. Certainly a definite written procedure for receiving and handling employee grievances will be established, and the procedure for carrying out performance evaluations will be carefully determined.

The steps that many supervisors or staff specialists perform do not need to be described in public procedural statements. Those processes (such as the determination of the salary scale) are part of the abilities of the person accomplishing the task and need not be formalized in writing.

A rule is defined as a law, regulation, or prescribed guide for conduct of action or behavior. Rules can be considered as minimum standards of conduct which apply to a group of people. Rules tend to apply uniformity to the group of people concerned.

Libraries, like all other institutions, must have rules. Examples of rules are the number of hours to be worked each week, rest periods, and behavior before the public. Rules serve to insure reasonable predictability of behavior so that the organization can achieve its goals and function without undue disruption.

As mentioned in Chapter 3, an organization sometimes develops too many rules. Employees become frozen; they have no freedom of action. Some rules are necessary, but too many are detrimental. It is often thought that rules tend to be established for that small group of employees who do not conform—those who do not observe, for example, the authorized length of a coffee break. The total group should not be penalized because of the action of a few.

UNIONIZATION

The history of labor's attempt to get fair and equitable treatment and to have a voice in the decisions that affect their lives goes back to the earliest days of the American colonies. In 1636 a group of Maine fishermen protested the withholding of their wages. The first local craft union was formed in Philadelphia in 1792 by shoemakers. The first national organization of workers that has continued to the present day is the Typographical Union, founded in 1752.[19] Labor continued to strive for better working conditions, shorter hours and better pay all thru the 1800s and early 1900s. Some of the conflicts between labor and management were violent, and many people were hurt or killed.

The federal government occasionally entered these conflicts through the establishment of Presidential Commissions which served as arbitrators or mediators. But only minor federal legislation was enacted until 1926, when the Railway Labor Act was passed establishing collective bargaining in the railway systems and procedures for the handling of grievances, arbitration, "cooling-off" periods, fact finding, and mediation.

But the real foundation of the American labor movement was laid in 1935, when the National Labor Relations Act, popularly known as the Wagner Act, was passed. This Act established the National Labor Relations Board and defined the right of workers to organize and to elect representatives to carry out collective bargaining. In the same year, the Social Security Act was established by Congressional action. In 1936, the Public Contract Act, the Walsh-Healy Act, established labor standards on government contracts including minimum wages, overtime, compensation for time over forty hours per week or eight hours per day.

The very important Labor Management Relations Act, better known as the Taft-Hartley Act, was passed in 1947; it amended some of the previously approved labor legislation, particularly the Wagner Act, but it also established certain union practices as unfair. The Taft-Hartley Act outlawed closed shops, jurisdictional strikes, sympathy strikes, and refusal to bargain. Also, it permitted states to pass "right-to-work" laws.

The Civil Rights Act was passed by Congress in 1964. Title VII of this Act prohibits discrimination in employment based on race, color, religion, sex, or national origin.

These, then, are keystones to labor relations today. After the passage of the Wagner Act in 1935, unions began to grow very rapidly. By 1970 union membership in the United States totaled 19,400,000. This membership constituted about 22.6 percent of the total work force and 27.4 percent of the employees in non-agricultural establishments. When employee associations engaging in collective bargaining are added, the figures increase to 21.3 million (24.7 percent and 30.1 percent, respectively).[20]

Historically most union activities have involved the blue collar worker. The craftsman, manual worker, and assembly line worker are included in the blue collar category. White collar workers were not much involved until the late 1950s. There is no clear definition of a white collar worker, but the Bureau of Labor statistics includes professional, technical, managerial, sales, and clerical workers in this category. Since 1956, however, the number of white collar workers included 17 percent of the total membership of national and international unions in the United States. When employee associations are added to unions, white collar membership rises to a total of 23 percent.[21]

Unions are presently focusing more attention on the white collar worker. Technological change in many industries has resulted in the reduction of the blue collar labor force. This has caused a slight decline in the number of union members. To compensate, many unions are concentrating on organizing the white collar worker. According to George Meany, president of the AFL-CIO, "organizing the unorganized" is considered the "greatest unresolved trade union problem."[22]

Because of the Taft-Hartley Act and some state right-to-work laws, unions find major problems in enforcing unionization. The closed shop (an industry or organization in which employers may hire only union members) is illegal, as is the union shop (where union membership is mandatory for all employees included in a bargaining unit). Because unions feel that individuals represented by the union should pay their share of union fees, maintenance of membership in a union is sometimes required during the period the contract is in force, unless state right-to-work laws prohibit the practice. Also, unless prohibited by state law, "agency shop" provisions may require non-union employees to pay a contribution to the union representing some employees of a unionized unit. Usually that contribution is equal to union dues.

Unionization of an organization may be accomplished in several ways: 1) Union organizers may start talking to employees while they are off the job about the benefits of unionization. 2) If a union represents part of the labor force of a specific organization, members of the unionized group or union organizers may talk to employees of non-unionized units. 3) Employees of a non-unionized organization who are dissatisfied with the policies and practices of the organization may solicit the help of an organizer or may submit a petition signed by at least 30 percent of the employees of the unit to the National Labor Relations Board.

If the employees initiating unionization action are successful in obtaining signatures of the required 30 percent of all employees of the unit being unionized, an election usually is held to determine the desire of all the employees to unionize and to determine the agency that will be designated the bargaining agent. A vote is not mandatory if the organization agrees to recognize a union as the bargaining agent. But such action leaves the designation of the bargaining agent unresolved, and it is open to challenge by both employees and other unions.

Only a simple majority of all employees concerned must be obtained to effect unionization. The election is carefully supervised by representatives of the National Labor Relations Board and procedures are carefully observed by management and union representatives to be sure no unfair labor practices are carried out. A number of provisions of the Taft-Hartley Act (as amended by the Labor-Management Reporting Act of 1959, the Handrum-Griffin Act) control unionizing campaigns.

After a union or employee association has been certified as the exclusive bargaining agent for a group of employees or for a total company, management and the union must bargain collectively. This action is required by the Taft-Hartley Act. Matters that will be discussed in the bargaining sessions include wages, hours, and other conditions of employment. Agreement on these matters must eventually be reached and a contract prepared which both sides are willing to sign and abide by for a stipulated time.

Generally, an organization designates one person as its representative to carry out the bargaining process and to represent management after the bargaining process. That person may be the library personnel officer, an industrial relations specialist, or any other individual delegated to represent management. The individual must understand the bargaining process, which, while not described here, is complex, frequently frustrating, and exhausting.

The bargaining group also appoint an individual to represent them, and after the labor contract is signed, to monitor management's actions to assure compliance with the contract. In industry this individual is known as the steward, or shop steward. It is to him that employees bring any complaints or grievances; it is with him that management must work closely to maintain labor's cooperation.

White collar workers, particularly professionals, have historically been reluctant to join unions. But in recent years teachers, nurses, and professionals in municipal, state, and federal employment are more actively participating in collective bargaining. At the present time all types of libraries are being affected by the movement of professionals to unionize.

Historically, the main reasons for unionization have been to effect better wages, fringe benefits, and working conditions. But other factors are influencing the professional. Employees today are demanding a greater voice in the administrative decisions that affect their lives. They are objecting to jobs that are prescriptive and that fail to allow for individual growth and professional movement. In frequent cases, unionization is brought on by the inept or irresponsible action of management. Unionization is sometimes seen as a way to maintain personal integrity and to assure fair and just treatment for oneself. So not all unionization activities are based on the desire for increased wages.

Managers of libraries must recognize that unionization will affect their organization and their method of management. As a result of the bargaining process and the signing of a labor contract, the power and authority of management sometimes is greatly reduced. The degree of power and authority that management loses will depend on the bargaining process. Some libraries, using inexperienced and untrained representatives at the bargaining table, lose so much authority that it becomes difficult to manage the institution. Others, because of more skilled negotiators, retain the power and authority to effect program direction, job definitions, and quality personnel programs.

Library managers frequently respond to unionization movements in a very negative way. They feel that the employees are ungrateful for management's attempts to improve working conditions. Managers feel hurt and consider employees disloyal to the goals of the organization. Such reactions, while perhaps natural, must be overcome. Good labor negotiations can occur only when management faces the problems calmly and objectively. After the negotiations are completed and a labor contract signed, the institution can best move ahead if there is a cooperative attitude between management and the union representation.

GRIEVANCES AND GRIEVANCE PROCEDURES

It was mentioned earlier that every library should have written personnel policies. These policies set forth standards for salary administration, promotion, transfer, demotion, termination, and other operational policies. In a non-unionized library, these policies are the guidelines for all supervisors. The statements are established to assure fair and equitable treatment of all workers. While personnel policy statements are formulated by management, the wise administrator will be sure not only that they are understood by the worker but also that the worker will understand why the policy has been established.

In a unionized organization, the personnel policies as modified by union-management negotiation become part of the union contract. A union contract usually spells out policies and procedures and workers' rights with respect to 1) wages and salaries; 2) hours of work; 3) holidays and vacations, demotions or force reduction, seniority, and policies of leaves of absence; 4) safety and health; 5) suspension and discharge; 6) training programs; and 7) the establishment of grievance channels.

Both the personnel policies developed by the organization and the policies and procedures established by a union contract are designed to guarantee fair treatment of workers. However, complaints and grievances will develop in spite of such precautions. Real or imagined unfair treatment of people will arise in any organization. Such feelings may vary from the supervisor's attitude toward an employee to the belief that promotion standards have not been fairly applied. Some workers harbor such feelings of unfair treatment within themselves. They are afraid to complain or express their unhappiness because of fear of reprisal by the supervisor. Other employees complain only to their immediate work group, thereby alienating the group from the supervisor. In either case, the individual or the group approaches the job with low morale and becomes a problem to the first-line supervisor.

One of the traditional ways of hearing and resolving employee grievances is the program known as the Open Door. This program is based on the assumption that when supervisors encourage employees to come to their office voluntarily at any time to discuss their problems and complaints, they will feel free to do so. But this assumption is not completely sound. The Open Door policy works only when the supervisor has been able to instill in the employee a feeling of trust. The employee must feel that his problem or complaint will be objectively heard and fairly resolved. He must feel that the supervisor will not hold it against him or consider him a troublemaker. If the Open Door program works, it is because the supervisor is particularly skilled in human relations and sensitive to employee needs and feelings. But such a program does give the supervisor opportunity to explain why certain action was taken and to resolve the complaint or grievance through direct communication.

The Open Door program, while it can operate in a unionized organization, is more likely to function in a non-unionized organization. With the absence of a union contract, the supervisor has more freedom and more alternatives available to him to resolve problems. Factual problems are probably the easiest to resolve, since they involve working conditions, hours of work, or changes in methodology of the job. But problems involving sentiment or feeling are much more difficult to handle. Here, the supervisor must constantly ask himself, "Why does the employee feel this way?" His answer will depend on his understanding of people.

Grievances in a unionized organization cannot be handled as directly as they are in the Open Door program. First, the union contract is the legal base for handling personnel grievances, and it must be adhered to. Second, a shop foreman is elected from the union membership. Although he is an employee of the company, the shop foreman is also the representative and spokesman for the union employees. Employee grievances are submitted to him rather than to the supervisor. The supervisor is generally on the defensive and frequently has difficulty in determining the facts of the situation. This is particularly true if the complaint involves sentiment and feeling. The supervisor has little opportunity to probe for the reason for such feeling. The problem is couched in factual and legalistic terms, sometimes hiding the real situation.

In this era, when the rights of employees are carefully protected, it is essential that organizations have a written, public grievance procedure. In a unionized organization this procedure will undoubtedly be part of the union contract. But in a non-unionized organization, management must see that such procedures are established. A grievance procedure defines 1) the manner in which grievances are filed (written or oral); 2) to whom the grievance is submitted; 3) how the grievance proceeds through the organization's hierarchy; 4) where decisions of resolution can be made; and 5) the final point of decision. Usually the procedures identify action the aggrieved employee can take if he is not satisfied with the final decision (such as appeal to the union membership or court action).

It must be kept in mind that grievance channels are ways of removing the employee from the direct and complete control of his immediate supervisor. Grievance channels discipline supervisors and act as a guarantee to employees. They exist to assure employees that justice is available and can be properly dispensed.

EMPLOYEE DISCRIMINATION

The history of the American effort to prohibit discrimination against certain groups of employees goes back to the Civil Rights Acts of 1866 and 1870 and the Equal Protection Clause of the 14th Amendment to the United States Constitution. Recent Presidents, including Eisenhower, Kennedy, Johnson, and Nixon, issued strong Executive Orders to prohibit discrimination in the United States Civil Service. President Eisenhower's Executive Order 10950 proclaimed "it is the policy of the United States Government that equal opportunity be afforded all qualified persons, consistent with law, for employment in the Federal Government." This was the first time the term "equal opportunity" surfaced. The concept of affirmative action was introduced in 1961. President Kennedy's Executive Order 10925 directed "positive measures for the elimination of any discrimination, direct or indirect, which now exists." President Johnson's Executive Order 11246 in 1965 introduced the significant charge of putting responsibility for government-wide guidance and leadership under the Civil Service Commission. President Nixon, soon after he took office in 1969, issued Executive Order 11478. This strong order made it clear for the first time that equal employment opportunity "applies to and must be an integral part of every aspect of personnel policy and practice in the employment, development, advancement, and treatment of civilian employees of the Federal Government." This Executive Order was considered a total integration of personnel management and equal employment opportunity in the federal government.

This movement in the United States Civil Service had an impact on other employers. And Congress, recognizing the need to guarantee equal employment opportunity, took action by passing the Civil Rights Act of 1964 (Public Law 88-352). Title VII, Equal Employment Opportunity, provides the basis for fair employment practices. This Title prohibits discrimination based on race, color, or national origin in all programs or activities that receive federal financial aid. This Act also established the Equal Employment Opportunity Commission as the agency to enforce this law.

In 1972 Congress amended the 1964 law by passing a stronger Equal Employment Opportunity Act, which greatly strengthened the power and expanded the jurisdiction of the Equal Employment Opportunity Commission. As amended, Title VII now covers 1) all private employers of fifteen or more persons; 2) all educational institutions, public or private; 3) state and local government; 4) public and private employment agencies; 5) labor unions with fifteen or more members; 6) joint apprenticeship and training.

The Equal Employment Opportunity Commission requires that all businesses, industries, and institutions under their jurisdiction prepare and have approved an Affirmative Action program to meet the requirements of the 1972 law. Recurring reports are required to show action taken and progress made. The Commission sets forth the following requirements for the Affirmative Action program:[23]

A. Issue a written equal employment policy and Affirmative Action commitment.
B. Appoint a Top Official with responsibility and authority to direct and implement your program.

1. Specify responsibilities of Program Manager.
2. Specify responsibilities and accountability of all Managers and Supervisors.
C. Publicize the policy and Affirmative Action commitment.
   1. Internally: To managers, supervisors, all employees and unions.
   2. Externally: To sources and potential sources of recruitment, potential minority and female applicants, to those with whom you do business, and to the community at large.
D. Survey present minority and female employment by department and job classification.
   1. Identify present areas and levels of employment.
   2. Identify areas of concentration and underutilization. An area of concentration is one in which there is a significant number of minorities or females. Underutilization is defined as having fewer minorities or women in a particular job category than would be reasonably expected by their presence in the relevant job market.
   3. Determine amount of underutilization.
E. Develop goals and timetables to improve utilization of minorities, males and females in each area where underutilization has been identified.
F. Develop and implement specific programs to achieve goals. This is the heart of the program. Review the entire employment system to identify barriers to equal employment opportunity; make needed changes to increase employment and advancement opportunities of minorities and females. These areas need review and action:
   1. Recruitment: All personnel procedures.
   2. Selection Process: Job requirements, job descriptions, standards and procedures. Pre-employment inquiries; application forms; testing; interviewing.
   3. Upward mobility system: Assignments; job progressions; transfers; seniority; promotions; training.
   4. Wage and salary structure.
   5. Benefits and conditions of employment.
   6. Layoff; recall; termination; demotion; discharge; disciplinary action.
   7. Union Contract Provisions affecting above procedures.
G. Establish internal audit and reporting system to monitor and evaluate progress in each aspect of the program.
H. Develop supportive in-house and community programs.

Other federal laws also strive to prohibit discrimination.

The Equal Pay Act of 1962 requires all employers subject to the Fair Labor Standards Act (FLSA) to provide equal pay for men and women performing similar work. In 1972, coverage of this Act was extended beyond employees covered by FLSA to an estimated fifteen million additional executives, administrators, and professional employees including academic and administrative personnel, teachers in elementary and secondary schools, and outside salespeople.

The Age Discrimination clause in the Employment Act of 1967 prohibits employers of twenty-five or more persons from discriminating against persons 40-65 years of age in any area of employment because of age.

FOOTNOTES

[1] William D. Halsey, ed., *Collier's Encyclopedia* (New York: Crowell Collier Educational Corp., 1972), vol. 8, p. 172.

[2] *American Libraries*, 6, no. 1 (January 1975): 39.

[3] *Standards for Accreditation, 1972* (Chicago: American Library Association, 1972), p. 5.

[4] It is interesting to note that this concept of skills is similar to the one used by Peter F. Drucker in his book *The Effective Executive* (New York: Harper and Row, 1967), Chapter 1.

[5] These examples of job descriptions were developed by participants in the HW funded institute, "Utilization of Library Manpower" held at the University of Denver, Graduate School of Librarianship, November 20-December 10, 1971 (John T. Eastlick, Director of the Institute).

[6] Maurice F. Tauber, and associates, *Technical Services in Libraries* (New York: Columbia University Press, 1959).

[7] Ernest De Prospo, Ellen Altman, and Kenneth E. Brashley, *Performance Measures for Public Libraries* (Chicago: American Library Association, Public Library Association, 1973).

[8] Lowell Martin, *Library Response to Urban Change* (Chicago: American Library Association, 1969).

[9] Note that, except for custodians, the levels identified are those included in the *Library Education and Manpower* policy statement of A.L.A.

[10] Denver Public Library, Librarian's Committee on Performance Evaluation, *Management Guide to Performance Evaluation* (1971), p. 1.

[11] Ibid., pp. 3-4.

[12] Denver Public Library, "Performance Evaluation." Reproduced with permission.

[13] Saul W. Gellerman, *Management by Motivation* (Chicago: American Management Association, 1968), p. 141.

[14] Carlyle Frarey, and Carol Learmont, "Placements and Salaries 1974; Promise or Illusion?", *Library Journal*, 100, no. 17 (October 1, 1975): 1767.

[15] *The Report of the National Commission on State Workmen's Compensation Laws* (Washington, D.C.: GPO, 1972), p. 15.

[16]*Equal Employment Opportunity Commission Guidelines on Discrimination Based on Sex* (Washington, D.C.: GPO; amended April 4, 1972).

[17]*Employee Benefits, 1971* (Washington, D.C.: Chamber of Commerce of the United States, 1971), p. 27.

[18]Ibid., p. 27.

[19]Wendell French, *The Personnel Management Process: Human Resources Administration*, 3rd ed. (Boston: Houghton Mifflin Company, 1974), p. 725.

[20]Bureau of National Affairs, *Labor Relations Yearbook—1972* (Washington, D.C.: Bureau of National Affairs, 1973), p. 296.

[21]Ibid.

[22]*Fortune*, 75, no. 2 (February 1967): 199.

[23]U.S. Equal Employment Opportunity Commission, *Affirmative Action and Equal Employment, a Guidebook for Employers*, Vol. 1 (Washington, D.C.: Superintendent of Documents, 1974), p. 16.

5

DIRECTING

Directing is that complex function of getting workers to perform tasks efficiently and effectively so that the goals and objectives of the organization are fulfilled. Directing is therefore concerned with the relationship of a supervisor to the subordinate at all levels of the organization.

Historically, the picture of supervision practices is not a pretty one. Most workers, history shows, have performed duties because they were forced to. They were coerced into accomplishing what was desired by their "masters." Threat of harm, fear of punishment, or dependence on the ruler for protection, food, and shelter were the motivators used for centuries. Slave of free man worked for the same reasons. Even when a strong and perhaps benevolent paternalism dominated the worker, that very attitude of paternalism reinforced his dependence on the father-figure and removed from him the power of making a decision, exercising judgment, or functioning as his own master.

Since the beginning of the Industrial Revolution, managers have used negative methods of getting workers to work. Managers have tried to keep the worker economically dependent. The threat of dismissal or demotion, with the resulting loss of income, has forced workers to perform. The fear of losing special benefits such as clean houses and schooling for children, as provided by Robert Owen's factory at New Lanark, dominated worker's thoughts. The total paternalism of Alfred Krupp lulled the worker into passive security. Economic dependence has been, and is today, a great motivator to get workers to work.

In recent years managers have added a new dimension to economic dependence. A form of bribery has developed. If workers exceed established standards, they are "awarded" trips at company expense, vacations at company-owned resorts at reduced rates, or special bonuses or gifts. Worker motivation, it is assumed, is increased through special awards.

The worker, whether man, woman, or child, has been considered a commodity comparable to other resources utilized by an industry or organization. The labor factor has dominated the human factor.

In the early 1900s, however, this attitude toward workers began to change. Both Frederick W. Taylor and Henri Fayol emphasized the worker's importance to an enterprise and pointed out that the supervisor had to understand workers and their motivations. Both urged cooperative and harmonious relationships between the two groups.

Directing, or supervising, or managing, then, is the complex process of getting things done through people. It is a manager's greatest challenge today, because patterns of supervision are shifting rapidly due to extensive research by the social scientist, the labor relations expert, and the industrial psychologist.

THE SUPERVISOR

Whether at the lowest level or the highest echelon of the organization, the supervisor is the key to the employees' attitudes toward their jobs and to the quality and quantity of productivity. Subordinate supervisors sometimes adopt the supervisory style they perceive their supervisor to exercise. But more frequently the supervisory style demonstrated by any supervisor is the product of his experience and his attitude toward people.

Some supervisors want to be considered "good guys." They want to be part of the group they must manage. Recently a major supervisor said, "I like to be considered one of the team, to joke with and tease the employees. But that sure creates a problem when I have to discipline, correct, or fire an employee." That statement illustrates the problem of the "buddy" supervisor.

Other supervisors maintain both a formal and informal distance between themselves and their employees. There is no on-duty socialization and no outside contact except at official office or company affairs. To the employee, such a supervisor seems distant, cold, and uninterested in his welfare. This supervisor probably feels that the responsibility of getting the department's work accomplished rests on his shoulders alone. No one else is concerned.

The two supervisors described above are extremes, it is granted. But both types are found in almost every organization. Both create problems for themselves and for the organization. Both cause trouble for their employees. An individual like the "good guy" changes when he has to discipline an employee; the "distant" supervisor breaks his barrier of isolation at the Christmas party. The behavior of both becomes inconsistent with the previous supervisory patterns.

Consistency of behavior is an essential characteristic of good supervisors. Those who show friendship and humor today and distance and aloofness tomorrow confuse the employee and undermine the relationship of the two people. The supervisor who loses his temper, "blows up," and causes a tense situation quickly loses his effectiveness as a supervisor. When an individual loses control of himself, performs actions which he normally would not perform, or says things which he shouldn't say, that individual is the loser—he has lost control in the fullest sense. He is inconsistent to the point that employees never know what to expect.

But consistency is not the only positive characteristic of a good supervisor. Studies made over the last several years have identified other attributes of the good supervisor.

The Hawthorne Studies

Between 1927 and 1932 Elton Mayo, of Harvard's Department of Industrial Research, made a study at the Hawthorne works of Western Electric Company in Chicago. This study has become a landmark in establishing in industry the modern concept of effective human relations. "The Hawthorne studies provide an excellent illustration of several important phenomena: restriction of output; informal work groups; the effects of the supervisor; and the so-called Hawthorne effect itself."[1]

As efficiency engineers at the Hawthorne plant were experimenting with various forms of illumination, an unexpected reaction from employees was noticed. When illumination was increased, productivity increased. That was not as surprising as the fact that when illumination decreased, production continued to increase. The same happened when the illumination wasn't changed at all. Mayo was asked to examine this paradox, and the "Hawthorne studies" resulted.

The study consisted of two parts. One involved special six-girl teams of workers. Working conditions for these teams were constantly changed to determine worker fatigue and worker production. Not only was the amount of illumination changed, but such factors as rest periods, shorter work days, coffee breaks, and other changes in standard working conditions were introduced. Employees had the authority to determine the timing of coffee breaks and could influence decisions relating to other changes. Mayo's conclusion was that "the singling out of certain groups of employees for special attention had the effect of coalescing previously indifferent individuals into cohesive groups with a high degree of group pride or esprit-de-corps."[2]

When a group develops pride in their work and has some degree of authority over their work habits, productivity increases. This is the famous "Hawthorne effect," which now is widely recognized and is applicable to many work situations.

The second part of the Hawthorne studies involved interviewing approximately 20,000 different workers. Two things soon became apparent from the interviews: 1) work in the factory was dismal and dull at best, and most employees accepted it passively and with a feeling of futility; 2) informal groups of workers emerged through which the worker acquired a feeling of belonging and being welcome. Management frequently considered these groups to be threats (which they were in some cases, for one of the primary functions of these groups was to provide a safe retaliation for poor managerial techniques). Slow-downs in production, poor or careless work, and the forcing of all workers to comply with the group's behavior were within the power of the group. But Mayo believed that the group could become a positive force for increasing productivity if management changed its attitude toward the group and used it for positive action.

For the supervisor, the importance of the Hawthorne studies is significant: 1) employees respond to managerial efforts to improve the working environment; 2) they respond to being capable of making decisions that affect their work patterns and job behavior; 3) the informal group can be a positive unit helping management to achieve its goals; 4) the informal group needs to develop a sense of dignity and responsibility and to be recognized as a constructive force in the organization; 5) the worker must feel that management needs and welcomes him.

Prudential Insurance Company of America

Soon after World War II, the University of Michigan established an Institute for Social Research. One of the companies this group studied was the Newark office of the Prudential Insurance Company of America.[3] The study, involving several large clerical departments, tried to identify supervisory styles of supervisors and their effect on employee productivity. It was recognized that a supervisor usually has a fairly clear and constant concept of his job. Because of this, the researchers could have the supervisor describe his job, identify objectives and obstacles to achieving those objectives, and discuss his personal methods of reaching those objectives.

The analysis of interview data made it possible to divide supervisors into three groups: predominantly production-centered supervisors, predominantly employee-centered supervisors, and mixed patterns. Because no one person is always the same, the word "predominantly" is important. A production-centered supervisor was one who felt full responsibility for getting the work done; his departmental employees were to do only what he told them to do. An employee-centered supervisor recognized that the subordinates did the work and that therefore they should have a major voice in determining how it was done. Coordinating and maintaining a harmonious environment was the supervisor's main responsibility.

The research results were surprising. Contrary to traditional management thinking, which emphasized that permissive supervision led to employee laxity and carelessness, the departments that had employee-centered supervisors had high production while those with production-centered supervisors produced less. The Michigan researchers had to make an assumption that was radical at the time and that is still surrounded by controversy: many workers like their jobs, they want to be productive, and they would be productive if given a share of control over their jobs.

Much research since the Prudential study supports the assumption made by the Michigan researchers, and the theory is applicable to many activities other than clerical activities. While it does not solve all supervisory problems, "the theory that workers feel responsible for productivity, and that employee-centered supervision is the best way to stimulate this feeling, has plenty of . . . evidence to support it."[4]

The Likert Theory of Supervision

Rensis Likert[5] in his book *New Patterns of Management* summarizes much of the research done at the Michigan Institute for Social Research up to 1961. It is a classic in the study of supervisory styles. Likert strongly rejects the theory that a concern for good human relations is a distraction to the primary function of management. He also rejects the theory that concern for good human relations reduces the efficient and profitable operation of an organization.

Likert recognizes that management's primary responsibility is to assure the best use of the organization's resources. Research has shown that strong centralized control of employees is not the best way to achieve operational efficiency or sustained productivity. A production-centered supervisory style may be detrimental to the organization's interest. There is no sentimentality involved in Likert's emphasis on human relations in supervision. He emphasizes that when management analyzes its operations, the appropriate supervisory style for the various operations can be determined. When the supervisor's style is attuned to the employee needs and job requirements, productivity is usually significantly higher and more constantly maintained. This is true for tasks that are worker-controlled; machine-controlled productivity jobs are dictated by the machine.

Likert in no way attempts to make a blanket prescription for employee-centered supervisory styles. He emphasizes that the supervisory methods used by supervisors in highly productive organizational units require "adaptability and adherence to a consistent appreciation of what the particular employees want and need rather than a doctrinaire insistence on being permissive."[6] Consistent productivity is the goal of any supervisor—not brief spurts of effort followed by a reduction of activities. Fluctuations in productivity frequently occur when employees receive pressure, threats, and constant watching by the supervisor. But this supervisory style brings its own destruction through the loss of morale and employee turn-over. It encourages production slow-downs, resistance to new methods, and strikes. Likert believes that pressure and strong control may have to be used in emergency situations, but that continual use of such techniques will not build good morale, good productivity, and a team spirit in an organization.

Research at the Institute for Social Research has proven that a feeling of responsibility toward one's work is natural and is any employee's general tendency. Supervisors can encourage this attitude of responsibility by demonstrating sincere respect for the employee's trustworthiness, intelligence, and knowledge of the job. The employee readily discerns any artificial declaration of faith, and his resultant distrust of the supervisor reduces his feelings of confidence and responsibility. But the supervisor who tries to reduce the number of restrictions placed on the employee, who is willing to consult with the employee about assigned tasks, and who makes sure the employee knows why a task is essential in the total flow of activity will strengthen that attitude of responsibility and develop good employees. Such a supervisor functions more as a partner in the activities of the organization than as a boss responsible for getting the job done.

The supervisor's success, then, will be determined by his supervisory style. Consistency in manner, a balance between over-friendliness and aloofness, a sincere respect for the employee's trustworthiness and intelligence, and a willingness to have the employee participate in making decisions that affect his job are attributes of the good supervisor. The good supervisor will not: 1) play favorites among employees, 2) apply rules and regulations differently to different employees, 3) develop in the employee a fear of the supervisor, and 4) make snap decisions with inadequate information.

MANAGEMENT PHILOSOPHIES

Any manager of people develops certain attitudes or philosophies about people in general and about workers specifically. His philosophy may develop from previous or current work experience, or because of the influence of the general work environment, and it colors the way in which a supervisor directs and evaluates workers. It determines the supervisor's opinion of what makes people work and what satisfactions, if any, they get from their job. The way in which a supervisor attempts to meet employee needs or to motivate employees is to a large extent determined by his philosophy of people.

These philosophies are probably assumptions about people and why they work. The assumptions are generally not provable; however, a number of social researchers have produced significant studies that need to be examined.

Maslow's Need Hierarchy

One of the important studies contributing to the understanding of people was accomplished by Abraham H. Maslow. He developed a hierarchy of human needs which, while not aimed primarily at work situations, is applicable to a work situation. The worker is viewed as moving from one level of need to another as his job develops. Five levels of need are identified by Maslow.[7]

I. Physiological needs
    The basic needs of any worker are food, water, shelter, sleep, which sustain life on its most minimal level.

II. Safety needs
    The worker needs an environment which provides an understandable, predictable and well-ordered situation. He needs assurance that the future physiological needs will be met. He is concerned about personal safety with security against theft, muggings, and attacks.

III. Social needs
    As other needs are met, the worker develops a need to belong, to love and be loved, to participate in activities which will create a feeling of togetherness.

IV. Esteem needs
    The worker desires respect from others, as well as having a high self-respect and self-esteem.

V. Growth needs
    At the highest level the individual achieves self-realization by performing at his maximum potential and strives to become everything that he is capable of becoming. He reaches self-actualization.

In any community or organization in the community, one can identify individuals who are at various levels of this need hierarchy. The hourly worker striving to maintain the basic physiological needs, the people in the urban center striving to find safety, the "joiners" of clubs, churches or social organization (the company bowling team), the head of the company who accepts the chairmanship of the United Way, the community leader who is a primary decision-maker for the community—these are examples of workers at different levels of the need hierarchy.

Of course, not everyone rises systematically up the need hierarchy. Sometimes an individual never has to be concerned with physiological needs because of affluent parents; others never rise above this point. It is sometimes said that only a very few people in the world have reached the fifth level, self-actualization. Mahatma Gandhi, Eleanor Roosevelt, and Winston Churchill are sometimes credited as having reached full self-actualization. It is believed, however, that many people achieve this level of self-realization. It may be that they have passed through the need for esteem from others and the need to belong to groups. They have the ability to live fully to their maximum potential without the trappings of other levels.

To a supervisor, the importance of Maslow's need hierarchy is that it gives a guide to an individual's needs and desires. By identifying an employee's current location on the hierarchy, the supervisor has a better basis for guiding, counseling, and advising the employee to growth performance. The supervisor must recognize that a satisfied need is not a motivator.

Douglas McGregor's Theory X and Y

Another group of assumptions about workers was developed by Douglas McGregor.[8] By using the symbols X and Y, he makes no symbolic difference between the assumptions. X and Y are simply labels to designate contrasting management assumptions. McGregor does not imply that all assumptions in either Theory X or Theory Y are always right or always wrong. They may change according to the realities of a specific organization. However, unrealistic assumptions about people have caused many good plans to fail. It a planned activity flies in the face of human nature, its success will be only as great as the non-human factors can insure. Not infrequently, when plans begin to fail management tightens controls and applies more pressure. McGregor found that such action only increases the potential for failure, for what is needed is a lessening of control and a freeing of initiative.

In 1960, McGregor defined Theory X as follows:

1) The average human being has an inherent dislike of work and will avoid it if he can.

This assumption is deeply imbedded in management thought. Management sees itself as responsible for obtaining "a fair day's work," reducing or stopping restriction on production and slowdowns.

2) Because of this human characteristic of dislike of work, most people must be coerced, controlled, directed, threatened with punishment to get them to put forth adequate effort toward the achievement of organizational objectives.

This assumption follows the concept of hard supervision as compared to soft (permissive-humanistic) supervision. The implication is that the dislike of work is so strong that more force than the promise of rewards must be exercised to get work accomplished.

3) The average human being prefers to be directed, wishes to avoid responsibility, has relatively little ambition, wants security above all.

Rarely is the "mediocrity of the masses" stated so bluntly as in this assumption. This concept is not generally verbalized in American society. But it has been a concept held by some managers.

The knowledge about human behavior in many specialized fields, however, has made it possible to create another generalization about the management of human resources. McGregor called this assumption Theory Y.

1) The expenditure of physical and mental effort in work is as natural as play or rest.

The average person does not basically dislike work, but may gain satisfaction from it or attempt to avoid it depending on past experiences.

2) External control and the threat of punishment are not the only means for bringing about effort toward organizational objectives. Man will exercise self-direction and self-control in the service of objectives to which he is committed.

3) Commitment to objectives is a function of the rewards associated with their achievement.

Such positive rewards as ego satisfaction and self-realization are the most significant and can be direct products of efforts directed toward organizational objectives.

4) The average human being learns, under proper conditions, not only to accept but to seek responsibility.

5) The capacity to exercise a relatively high degree of imagination, ingenuity, and creativity in the solution of organizational problems is widely, not narrowly, distributed in the population.

6) Under the conditions of modern industrial life, the intellectual potentialities of the average human being are only partly utilized.

These assumptions are much more challenging to management strategy. They are dynamic, not static. They indicate that human beings have the possibility of growing and developing. Most importantly, it makes management responsible for creating an environment that will permit the positive development of its human resources.

McGregor was the leading spokesman for the behavioral approach to management. He had both strong support for his philosophy and opponents to his concepts, and he persisted in expanding his assumptions about human beings. In 1966[9] he stated the concepts of Theory X in a slightly different way, but a way that still emphasizes the negative approach to supervision:

1) Management is responsible for organizing the elements of productive enterprise (money, materials, equipment, people) in the interest of economic ends.

2) With respect to people, this is the process of directing their efforts, motivating them, controlling their actions, modifying their behavior to fit the needs of the organization.

3) Without this active intervention by management, people would be passive—even resistent—to organizational needs. They must therefore be persuaded, rewarded, punished, controlled; their activities must be directed. This is management's task in managing subordinate managers and workers.

4) The average man is by nature indolent; he works as little as possible.

5) He lacks ambition, dislikes responsibility, prefers to be led.

6) He is inherently self-centered, indifferent to organizational needs.

7) He is by nature resistant to change.

8) He is gullible, not very bright, the ready dupe of the charlatan and the demagogue.

The human side of economic enterprise today is fashioned from propositions and beliefs such as these. Conventional organization structures, managerial policies, practices, and programs reflect these assumptions. However, this still seems a very pessimistic assessment of the average worker. It certainly is an unflattering one that many workers and supervisors would challenge. But the beliefs are stated as assumptions held by some managers. In some cases they may be true and in others false; assumptions as such have no proof. If they are true, then a supervisor with Theory X personnel would have to find a supervisory style that would get the work performed effectively. Whether he used a soft approach or a hard approach to supervision, there would be difficulty.

McGregor modified the Theory Y concept as follows:[10]

1) Management is responsible for organizing the elements of productive enterprise (money, materials, equipment, people) in the interest of economic ends.

2) People are *not* by nature passive or resistant to organizational needs. They have become so as a result of experience in organizations.

3) The motivation, the potential for development, the capacity for assuming responsibility, the readiness to direct behavior toward organizational goals are all present in people. Management does not put them there. It is a responsibility of management to make it possible for people to recognize and develop these human characteristics for themselves.

4) The essential task of management is to arrange organizational conditions and methods of operation so that people can achieve their own goals best by directing their own efforts toward organizational objectives.

While Theory Y is not diametrically opposed to Theory X, it still presents a much more positive picture of people. According to this assumption, people are the product of their past experiences, their behavior can be modified or changed, and they can be motivated to work and assume responsibility. Within the philosophy expressed in Theory Y, it is management's job to develop work assignments that are challenging to the worker and that help the worker to achieve his personal goals and objectives. At the same time, such work assignments must contribute to the accomplishment of management's goals and objectives.

If a supervisor accepts the assumptions set forth in Theory Y, his supervisory style will reflect a different set of values than would be demonstrated in Theory X. A greater respect for people as human beings would be demonstrated. Although he would not be exercising a soft or permissive form of supervision, the supervisor would be more participative in decision-making and more cognizant of the workers' needs.

The Economic and the Social Man

Following McGregor, increased attention has been given to the study of man's behavioral patterns. New and more detailed studies have resulted in new assumptions about man. Schein identifies four conceptions about man in the order of their historical appearance. Assumptions deduced from the concept of a rational economic man are:

1) Man is primarily motivated by economic incentives and will do that which gets him the greatest economic gain.

2) Since economic incentives are under the control of the organization, man is essentially a passive agent to be manipulated, motivated, and controlled by the organization.

3) Man's feelings are essentially irrational and must be prevented from interfering with his rational calculations of self-interest.

4) Organizations can and must be designed in such a way as to neutralize and control man's feelings and therefore his unpredictable traits.

It is not known when these assumptions about man were formulated. Shein does not identify those by whom they are held to be true. But the concept of the "economic man" is interesting and observable in modern society. Probably these assumptions were formulated before the Hawthorne studies, because assumptions coming from those important studies define man as a social creature.

The concept of the social man is:

1) Man is basically motivated by social needs and obtains his basic sense of identity through relationships with others.

2) As a result of the Industrial Revolution and the rationalization of work, much of the meaning has gone out of work itself and must therefore be sought in the social relationships on the job.

3) Man is more responsive to the social forces of the peer group than to the incentives and controls of management.

4) Man is responsive to management to the extent that a supervisor can meet a subordinate's social needs and needs for acceptance.

Whether man is the indolent creature suggested by McGregor, an economically motivated creature, or a creature dominated by social needs is still a question. These are all assumptions about man's nature. A supervisor, whether in industry or in a library, must develop his own philosophy of human nature.

Koontz and O'Donnell recognize that man has superimposed an intelligence upon his animal nature and thus has modified his behavior. His mind and conceptual ability makes it possible for him to create an imaginative world, to exercise a degree of foresight, and to modify and direct his basic nature so that needs and satisfactions can be achieved. Koontz and O'Donnell[12] indicate that

this view of the nature of man makes it possible to deduce certain conclusions that are of the utmost importance to the manager. These may be listed as follows:

1) The individual is the primary concern of man.

Man looks after himself both in the extremities of life or death and in the modern affluent society. It is he who wants preferment, who wants to win. He may very well enjoy the success of other after he has achieved, although his jealous and skeptical nature shows through. True, we do have our unselfish heroes, men who willingly have laid down their lives for others, the wholly unselfish mother, the man who will step aside for the benefit of others. The rarity of these people makes them subject to comment and to award.

2) The individual will work to satisfy the demands of his basic nature if the benefits exceed the costs.

It is often said that man enjoys work. This is certainly true if the effort is directed toward satisfying the demands of his complex nature. He is doing this even when he tinkers. As he approaches the point of marginal satisfaction, he scarcely has the will and verve to apply himself to the specific labor *for the same reason*. For instance, he may work at his bench with unusual productivity in order to save time at the end of the day to experiment with a new tool or a new method he has invented. In this view, the objective work may change for the worker several times a day.

3) The individual can be led.

Man responds to leadership. He can be persuaded through many devices to take the desired road, but the devices themselves must be selected, tuned, and timed to the individual's need to satisfy his basic nature. Appeals to pride, status, greed, and many other aspects of man's nature are sometimes successful. Ancient armies were led with promises of booty; modern armies would have none of this. The leader must be intuitive in identifying the persuasive device to which another, at a given time, will respond positively.

4) The individual wants to live and work in a social environment.

This seems to be true most of the time. There is a definite need for solitude, however; sometimes people cannot bear people; many scientists still work best alone. In general, these periods of time are much shorter than those when man desires group associations. Both aspects rest squarely upon man's basic nature. Man may be largely a social animal, but he is not entirely so.

5) The individual helps to create institutions to serve the needs of their memberships.

There are many needs that man alone cannot satisfy. He can achieve them only through cooperative effort. If they promise a surplus of benefits over costs, he is likely to accept the implied limitations upon his individuality. For these reasons man creates government, educational, religious, health, and many other institutions. His chief problem in large-scale society is to retain his mastery of the institutions he has created and not become their slave.

6) There is no average man.

Attempts to take the square root of mankind, on the assumption that people are all alike, are bound to fail. People are not all alike. Natures are different and, for the individual, his nature may differ from time to time. Man does not, even as an individual, proceed to accommodate all aspects of his basic nature in the same degree at a given time. He exhibits priorities and these are kaleidoscopic.

7) The individual rises to the challenge of his full capabilities.

Man is impatient to use his abilities to their fullest extent. He resents the lack of opportunities to apply his knowledge and skills and to shoulder the responsibility for results. He becomes bored working at half speed, with routine. He is curious to learn the maximum level of his capabilities and he wants to operate at this level.

THE SUPERVISOR AND MOTIVATION

Around the world people work. They expend effort to achieve some goal. The goal may be of little value or of high scientific or cultural significance, but energy is put forth to accomplish a task. If, as McGregor indicates in Theory X, work is unnatural and repugnant to man, why are millions of people involved in work?

In many cultures work is a group activity. Entire families or groups of families cooperate in growing and harvesting food. All of the men of the group participate in the defense of the group. The pressure of the group causes some people to work perhaps harder and more conscientiously or perhaps slower and at the group's tempo. Group pressure is a strong motivating force, as identified in the Hawthorne studies. Not to be of the group is to lose social contact with one's peers. The social man, as discussed earlier, needs the group and the social contacts and safety it offers.

All organizations are composed of units established to perform specific tasks. While these units vary in size, each has its own supervisor. Each unit is in reality a group of workers striving to achieve specific goals and objectives. Many supervisors look at their subordinates as individuals, each of whom has his own problems and attitudes. They forget that these employees constitute a group and that the group can be used positively to help establish and achieve the unit's goals and objectives.

New theories of motivation place much emphasis on the power of groups to make workers want to work. Likert disagrees with the kind of organizational charts presented in Chapter 4. He believes that each organizational unit functioning as a group must interrelate with other groups until it becomes one large group all striving to achieve common goals.[13] Thus, the organization becomes an integrated whole. Likert says "an organization will function not as individuals but as members of highly effective work groups with high performance goals."[14] A supervisor following this philosophy should deliberately endeavor to build these effective groups, linking them into an overall organization by means of people who hold overlapping group membership.

It is this philosophy of supervision that has led to such developments as participative management, where the group has the power of decision-making. Also, since the goals of the group are determined by group decisions, each individual tends to have a high degree of ego identification with the goals and will strive harder to achieve them. His motivation to achieve is increased. This is the psychological base for Gellerman's *Management by Motivation*.[15] Man is motivated to work if he views his supervisor as supportive, fair, and constructive, and if he is able to maintain his sense of personal worth and importance.

For the group (but the theory is also applicable to an individual) Odiorne proposes that motivation can be accomplished by establishing, in cooperation with the group, specific objectives to be achieved.[16] But the process by which the objectives are achieved is not determined. Process is left to the group to determine—subject, of course, to quality control and to restrictions of space, time, and equipment. Odiorne's philosophy of motivation may be more easily applied to individuals, but numerous demonstrations, such as the Volvo experiment of worker groups responsible for the total assembling of a car, prove that it is applicable also to groups.

But not all individuals work in groups. Many work as individuals even in large organizations. It is evident that their motivation is not primarily social but dominantly economic. At first, motivation may be the necessity of meeting those basic physiological needs identified by Maslow. The needs for food, shelter and clothing are recurring, constant needs. Hunger is a great motivator, causing people not only to work but in some situations to commit numerous and varied crimes!

But in America, the assurance of food, shelter, and clothing is not enough. This society, which is strongly materialistic, seeks more than the minimal creature comforts. Man seeks other things that require money—and money comes from work. Man strives to earn more in order to satisfy needs and desires beyond the physiological requirements. Money is a great motivator. Success is frequently measured according to the amount of money earned or accumulated.

Money itself is not the major motivator, however, according to studies accomplished by Frederick Herzberg and his associates.[17] In the book *The Motivation to Work*, an extensive study is reported showing that an individual's morale affects his attitude toward work. High morale indicates a high job-attitude; low morale indicates a low attitude toward a job. Morale can thus be defined as the attitude with which an employee approaches his job. Herzberg developed a questionnaire which required lengthy descriptive reports of events which made the worker feel good or bad. The answers were analyzed to identify the elements of high job-attitudes. Middle management personnel in a large diversified construction company were used as the testing group.

The analysis of data showed that the most frequent factor in a high job-attitude is achievement. Success in the completion of a job created the highest job-attitude. Beginning with achievement, factors that were identified are ranked here from high to low:

1) Achievement
2) Recognition by supervisors, peers, or customers and subordinates of work accomplished.
3) Work itself—aspects of the job that gave the worker personal satisfaction.
4) Responsibility—being able to work without supervision and being responsible for one's own effort.
5) Advancement—a promotion indicates growth, recognition, achievement, and more responsibility.

The five factors above all relate to the job itself. They do not relate to other factors found by Herzberg to be characteristics of the context or environment in which the job is done. The other factors that influence high job-attitudes are:

6) Salary
7) Possibility of growth
8) Interpersonal relations (subordinate)
9) Status
10) Interpersonal relations (superior)

11) Interpersonal relations (peer)
12) Supervision
13) Company policies and administration
14) Working conditions
15) Personal life
16) Job security

Herzberg emphasizes the differences between the first five factors, which relate to the actual job, and the last eleven, which describe the job situation and which he identified as hygienic factors. The factors that seem to have a long-range effect on job attitudes are work itself, responsibility, and advancement. However, achievement and recognition as factors for high job attitudes are of shorter duration. The combining of some of these factors (such as advancement and recognition) is a strong factor in developing a high job attitude.

For many people achievement alone creates a positive attitude toward work. To achieve—to complete a project or assignment—brings fulfillment and personal satisfaction. Even if there is no recognition for achievement, a worker knows within himself that he accomplished the job. Some recognition will increase his job satisfaction. Even a verbal recognition or a pat on the back will increase for a short time his job satisfaction.

In Herzberg's study a salary increase is a motivator, but one that lasts only a short time. The effect of a salary increase is soon dissipated. It does not have the long-range effect that achievement and recognition provide.

Since Herzberg's landmark study, many other studies on motivation have been conducted. Some, much to the surprise of the researchers, have shown over and over that money and security are the primary motivators for getting workers to produce. It is possible that motivators change as world and national situations change. Could it be that security becomes dominant when jobs are scarce and the holding of a job is vital? But when jobs are plentiful, security is not as strong a motivator. The same could be said about money as a motivator. Rising prices and inflation put an emphasis on money, while a stable economy removes the pressure of money as a strong motivator.

It is the supervisor's job to build into his supervisory style behavioral patterns that will motivate the worker to perform tasks efficiently. There is no prescription that can be offered to assure success. Rather, each supervisor has to evolve his own pattern in view of his personality, his managerial philosophy, and his knowledge of the worker. The efficient supervisor will take advantage of the worker's personal and environmental reasons for working and will add identified additional inducements for working. Thus, a system of motivation emerges rather than a single source of motivation. Some inducements to work may be negative, but the majority will be positive. A system of inducements is not designed for across-the-board application but rather is designed to permit workers to select those inducements which provide the best motivation for them.

A sound motivational system is based on sociological principles, the policies of the organization, and the supervisor's philosophy of man's needs. Primary in any motivational system is the organization's responsibility to satisfy employee needs. This is difficult to accomplish because the needs of human beings not only vary greatly but also are flexible and subject to change. Perhaps the best a supervisor can do is to satisfy the most common needs of workers. Maslow's hierarchy of needs give the supervisor a good guide of a range of needs, from basic life requirements to the social, ego, and creative needs. Likert and others emphasize the power of the group. Herzberg's studies show the need for recognition, achievement, advancement, and responsibility. Other studies emphasize the need for increased monetary rewards and job security.

The policies of the organization should be structured so that the capacity to do good work—work of growing significance—is not stifled. Good productivity reflects the employee's quality of motivation.

Frequently the goals and objectives of an organization will spark an employee. He wants to be part of and contribute to their achievement. A high degree of achievement of its goals and objectives reflects well on the organization, creating a positive image of it. The worker is proud to be part of that organization and is motivated to promote its success through efficient work.

Also vital to any system of motivation is the quality of worker selection and training. It is obvious that the capable and well-trained employee will be a more productive employee. The organization must plan a sound orientation and training program. Training is discussed in detail later in this chapter.

Any system of motivation, then, depends on the supervisor. The manner in which he applies his knowledge of employee needs and desires, the organizational environment that releases the capacity for work, the quality of training received by capable employees, and the pride of the employee in the organization for which he works establish the basic climate of the motivational system. It is the supervisor's responsibility to exercise sound judgment to make the system work. The system works when there is good productivity, high morale, a friendly, competitive team spirit, and a dedication to the organization's goals and objectives.

THE SUPERVISOR AND LEADERSHIP

Webster's dictionary defines a leader as a "guide, conductor, chief or head of a group." That definition implies that a leader is part of a group but is apart from the group because of leadership responsibilities. The leader never loses his individual identity, though he acts to help the group achieve its goals and objectives. Carter gives five definitions of leadership:[18] 1) polarization of members of a group around some central person; 2) the person able to direct a group toward its goals; 3) the person selected by group members to lead them; 4) the person able to move a group along a specific dimension; and 5) the person possessing certain behavior patterns and capabilities.

In all definitions given above one person is designated the leader. This has been true historically for many centuries. Without one position that represents authority and gives direction, organizations tend to disintegrate. When two or more individuals try to fulfill the leadership role, the organization, because of conflicting direction, becomes formless and unable to act. Therefore, the basic concept of the superior-subordinate in an organization is established. The superior-subordinate group concept provides for the interlinking of groups through the scalar chain of authority of the organization. It is through this interlinking of the superior-subordinate group that the leader can direct action, effect change, and depend on subordinates for effective supportive endeavors.

It is true that in some libraries in recent years experiments in management have been conducted to place the power of direction in the hands of committees or a group of supervisors. This is, of course, in violation of the superior-subordinate concept described above. As mentioned earlier, such managerial experiments have been called "participative management." The designated authority group makes the decisions that give direction to the institution.

In libraries, leaders at any level of the hierarchy are either promoted or appointed to their positions of leadership. The function of leadership assigned to an individual cannot be abnegated or eliminated. Though delegation of certain leadership functions might occur, the end responsibility for the direction of an organization or, at a lower level, of a group of employees, still rests with the one to whom the leadership role was assigned. Participative management is good in the sense that the leader seeks the advice and counsel of associates and then makes a decision in light of that advice. However, participative management in the sense that a group makes decisions is dangerous to the institution and represents a failure of the designated leader to accept his responsibility.

Each leader must develop his own style of leadership. Some leaders may be "soft" or extremely permissive. Employees are given little direction and generally few decisions are made by the supervisor. The group of employees seems to "drift along." Social psychologists have found that some groups function well under this form of supervision, particularly if they know their job well and are dedicated to the accomplishment of their responsibility. But most groups functioning under extremely permissive leadership tend to disintegrate. Their tasks are not fulfilled and tensions develop because various members of the group want to deviate from established goals or processes. Occasionally a member of a group receiving this type of supervision will assume the leadership role, pulling the group back into a productive unit but relegating the assigned supervisor to an untenable position.

The opposite supervisory style is that identified as "autocratic." Here the leader functions as a total dictator, prescribing every action and activity. This "hard" leadership discourages creativity and communication. Employees generally respond in a retreat to silence, passiveness, and resignation. They perform the tasks they have to, but no more.

These are, of course, descriptions of leadership roles at each end of the spectrum. Most leaders are somewhere in the middle of these extremes. The trend is for leaders to adopt a more humanistic attitude toward employees and to involve them in activities, studies, and decisions that affect their jobs.

A good leader of a library will develop a group of counselors or advisors through whom he receives information. Such groups will include staff, the constituency, and governing boards. The complexities of a large library are so great that generally no one leader can anticipate all the ramifications and side effects his decisions might have. So the wise leader will involve those people who will be affected by decisions in the decision process.

Decision making is expected of a leader. The subordinates expect and have the right to anticipate decisions that will affect them and their work. The constituency of a library has the right to expect the leader to make decisions concerning the quality of library service available to them. Decision making is a primary responsibility of the leader. But the process of making decisions is not easy. Snap decisions usually are bad or at best very risky because they are not based on fact. The gathering of all possible facts about a problem is the first step of decision making. Second, all possible solutions or alternatives must be identified. The wise leader evaluates each alternative in the light of possible reaction. As discussed in Chapter 2, this process of attempting to forecast the effect of a decision is a vital step. Only after such careful studies does the wise leader make a decision.

The astute leader will establish short- and long-range goals for the institution, develop specific objectives to accomplish those goals, and develop programs to meet the objectives. He will constantly be evaluating and restructuring the organization so that goals and objectives can be achieved. This responsibility, as creative as that of establishing goals, "means shaping the character of the organization, sensitizing it to ways of thinking and responding so that increased reliability in the expectation and elaboration of plans will be achieved according to its spirit as well as its letter."[19]

The leader of a library, while accomplishing the processes of planning, organizing, staffing, and controlling, will establish written policies for the guidance of subordinate supervisors. A policy is a written statement setting forth a decision that directs present and future action. Such policy statements maintain consistency and continuity. Policy statements should in general emphasize "what is to be done," not procedurally "how it is to be done." Such statements are readily available to all staff members.

Emphasis has been placed on the role of the leader in the process of directing an institution. The leader has other functions, which are just as important. The manner in which the leader will fulfill the functions of being responsive to staff and constituency requests and of representing the institution locally as well as regionally and nationally will depend to a large degree on his personality and attitude toward people. But these functions are part of the responsibilities of a leader and must be fulfilled. To a large degree, the image an institution creates is determined by the leader who is the directing force of that institution.

Any leader working within an organization has to be careful that his effectiveness is not dissipated by organizational restrictions. An organization is supposed, through the unification effort, to strengthen the effectiveness of a leader. But frequently organizational obstacles are placed in the leader's way. Drucker identifies four obstacles to a leader's effectiveness:[20]

1) The executive's time tends to belong to everyone else. (The leader has difficulty in controlling his time because of the organizational responsibility to be available to staff and constituency.)

2) Executives are forced to keep on "operating" unless they take positive action to change the reality in which they live and work. (Direct control of organizational units dominates the leader's time and prohibits him from functioning as a coordinator, motivator, and creator.)

3) The leader is pushed toward ineffectiveness because he is within the *organization*. (He is effective only when other people make use of what he can contribute.)

4) The leader is *within* the organization. (The organization is seen only from inside; the organization from the outside is seen only through distorted lenses. What actually goes on is seen only through reports, statistics, and second-hand information. The leader must get outside and view the organization as it really is.)

A leader who controls his time, contributes to the endeavor of the organization, and sees the institution in reality will undoubtedly be an effective, dynamic leader.

THE SUPERVISOR AND COMMUNICATION

Most supervisors spend a large share of their time communicating with other people. Indeed, some studies show that 60 percent to 100 percent of a supervisor's time is spent carrying out this process. It is apparent, then, that communication is an important element of supervision.

Communication between individuals and groups is as old as recorded history. Yet it is only recently that the topic of communication has emerged in management literature. C.I. Bernard[21] was one of the first and best-known authorities to give serious consideration to problems of communication. He defined communication as the means by which people were linked together in an organization in order to achieve a central purpose. More recently the American Society of Training Directors has defined communication as the interchange of thought or information to bring about mutual understanding and confidence or good human relations. It appears, then, the communication is the exchange of words, letters, symbols, or messages in such a way that one individual or group receives information and understanding from other individuals or groups. It must be emphasized that the transfer of information is not nearly as difficult as the transfer of understanding. Understanding is achieved when the relevance of the transferred information is recognized as pertinent to the achievement of organizational goals.

Warren Weaver and Claude Shannon view communication as occurring in a system:[22] an information source (person or machine) selects a desired message from a set of possible messages; the selected message is then changed into a form to be transmitted over the communication channel to the receiver; the receiver changes the transmitted signal back into a message. Wolf simplifies this system with the following example: You ask a friend to open the door: your brain is the information source, your friend's brain is the destination, your vocal system is the transmitter, the sound waves serve as the principal channel of communication, and your friend's ear is the receiver.[23]

Actually, this sounds like a very simple system, but in practice it is seldom precise. The signal selected by the information source may be the wrong one, the signal transmitted may not give the intended information, the message may be distorted by unwanted additions or omissions while being sent or received. All such alterations in the transmitted signal are called "noise" in communications theory.

The majority of all communication involves symbols. The most frequent form of communication is carried on through a variety of codified symbols. Such symbols are languages—English, French, German, etc. Each consists of a plurality of signs that have a known meaning in written or oral form to a number of people, and the signs (written and oral) are capable of being reproduced. Written and oral communication based on a language is the most frequent form of communication used. However, actions, objects, and signs (since they, too, may have a known interpretation to a number of people and can be reproduced) often constitute communication languages. Jurgen Ruesch and Weldon Kees describe these languages as follows: [24]

Sign language: "Sign language includes all forms of codification in which words, numbers, and punctuation marks have been supplanted by gestures; these may vary from the 'monosyllabic' gestures of the hitch-hiker to such complete systems as the language of the deaf."

Action language: Action language "embraces all movements that are not used exclusively as signals. Such acts as walking and drinking, for example, have a dual function: on the one hand they serve personal needs, and on the other they constitute statements to those who may perceive them."

Object language: Object language "comprises all intentional and nonintentional display of material things, such as implements, machines, art objects, architectural structures, and last but not least, the human body and whatever clothes cover it."

Through the use of these various languages, then, the supervisor communicates with his subordinates, his peers, and superiors. He writes memos, letters, and policy manuals; he holds meetings with individuals and groups to discuss programs and problems; he observes sign, action, and object language and interprets the meaning of such language. And the good supervisor does one other thing in the communication process. He listens. In oral communication he listens not only to the message being sent—what is being said—but also he listens for the true meaning of what is being said. These other languages will occasionally help distinguish the true message from the false.

While an individual cannot resist being influenced by action, object, and sign languages, it is to verbal language—written and oral—that most attention is given. Most people, and certainly librarians, spend most of their day responding to verbal languages. Words (spoken, read, or thought) dominate.

Sometimes there are too many words. A supervisor must expect that there will be various forms of communication from his subordinates. Specifically designed, required reports are needed for decision-making. Suggestions, complaints, and commendations come from subordinates. The supervisor in actual practice receives information not only from subordinates, but from superiors and from external sources. Sometimes he receives too much information. No one yet has been able to answer adquately the question "How much information do I need?" But useless or unimportant information is noise in the communication process and distracts from the significant message.

In any organization communication is a two-way process. The good supervisor operates on the theory that the informed employee is a good employee. The supervisor assures the transmittal of information through the hierarchy according to authority lines. This formal channel of communication requires written memos, directives, and policy statements. It is hoped that these written statements not only answer "what" but also "why." The "why" gives understanding to the employee and the "what" gives the information. But written communication has numerous problems. Some may be poorly written and may not fully explain the action desired or completely define the scope of the problem. Employees are left with ambiguous instructions. Words used in written communications are frequently unclear and not defined. Every profession has its own vocabulary, and the same word may have several meanings. In librarianship, the word "system" has at least three meanings. Written communication allows no opportunity for feed-back and clarification. The subordinate employee must interpret the message to the best of his ability, and his perception is based on his past experience and present needs.

Oral communication conducted through individuals or groups also has problems. Not all oral messages are clearly stated. There is still the problem of the ambiguous or misunderstood word. But in oral communication there is an opportunity for discussion—feedback—through which clarification can be accomplished. Frequently oral communication is the best way to resolve conflict situations. Organizations should not be afraid of conflict situations if the issues are faced on an intellectual rather than an emotional basis. After oral communication has occurred between individuals or groups, it is not unusual for written communication to be prepared that summarizes the agreements, conclusions, or resolutions reached through the oral communication. Oral communication provides an excellent opportunity for the supervisor to observe the employee's use of object language, particularly as expressed by the body. Body language involves the use of gestures, tone of voice, facial expression, and, perhaps most important, eye expression and contact.

What has been discussed so far is the upward and downward formal pattern of communication in an organization. The messages are sent up or down the hierarchical lines of authority. However, a supervisor must recognize and encourage horizontal lines of communication. These informal channels through which peers communicate provide opportunities not only for clarification but also for coordination of effort. A supervisor should not fear these informal channels but should encourage them. Social events, coffee breaks, and informal staff meetings provide opportunities for such informal communication.

When formal communication is inadequate and events occur within an organization that are unexplained or hidden, it is not unusual for rumors and false information to enter the informal communication channels. The "grape-vine" makes its appearance. Rumor tends to develop in an organization in proportion to the importance and ambiguity of its subject matter in the lives of the individual members of the group. While some rumors start as idle gossip or surface social communication, most rumors circulate because they provide an explanation for individuals and groups and provide a release for the emotional tensions felt by individuals. As rumors spread they tend to become shorter and more concise. Each individual involved in communicating a rumor injects into the rumor such falsification and distortion as is consistent with his feelings, thinking, perceiving, and acting. Rumors can be stopped by clear, concise, complete communication through the formal communication channels.

Each supervisor must establish his own program of communication. For the downward flow of information, he might use memos, letters, bulletin boards, staff newspapers, published reports such as annual reports, or employee handbooks and policy manuals. For the upward flow of information the supervisor might encourage suggestion systems, group discussions, listening carefully to grievances and the grape-vine, face-to-face meetings with employees at different levels of the organization, and attitude surveys. Regardless of the methods selected, the message carried in communication must always be as clear and precise as possible and there should be provision for feedback.

THE SUPERVISOR AND EMPLOYEE TRAINING

Almost all practicing librarians today have some assigned responsibilities that involve the training of other employees. The trainee may be a shelver or beginning clerical employee, or he may be another professional. Regardless of the level, training has to be accomplished. As a professional librarian assumes a great role as manager, training will be one of his major responsibilities.

The concept of training can be limited to instructing an individual in specific steps that are essential for achieving a coordinated, uniform product. Or training can be on as broad a spectrum as a presentation of the philosophies and techniques essential to make a community analysis. Here, the term training is intended to cover the total gamut of instructing individuals, not only in how to do a job but also in why an assigned job is important. An employee performing a task without understanding why it is important and how it fits into the total endeavor of the institution probably will perform perfunctorily at best. If the employee understands and appreciates why a job is assigned, he will probably perform more efficiently.

In a library, as in any institution, there are many levels of training. Some training everyone receives; other parts of the training program are more individualized. The importance of training is based on the assumption that the informed employee is a good employee. With that assumption in mind the following training programs are suggested. Some libraries will be able to utilize all suggested activities, while others will use only a few because training is expensive in time. But over a period of time, the cost to the institution is returned in quality performance.

General Orientation

Soon after an employee has been hired, a general orientation meeting is held. This general orientation for all employees, regardless of level or place of employment within the institution, is designed to provide general information that all must have. Perhaps some of the information has been transmitted during the employment process. But is wise to reinforce that knowledge. A general orientation can be planned so that two basic areas are covered—general information and the goals, objectives, and philosophies of the organization.

This part of the orientation covers rules and policies applicable to all employees, including information concerning pay periods, how vacation and sick leave are accumulated and how they can be used, requirements for reporting illness, and the use of time clocks. Many libraries have specific ways of answering telephone calls, such as requiring that the name of the library (or department) and the individual's name be given. The reason for this requirement should be explained. Many libraries require employees to wear name tags. Again, the reason for this is given. The overall policies and rules that affect all employees are interpreted—not in a manner of constraint but rather in a style that will make the new employee feel a part of the organization and sympathetic with general requirements.

Each employee, regardless of level or place of employment in the institution, needs to know the overall goals, objectives and basic service philosophies of the organization. These are carefully and thoroughly presented by a major manager of the organization. If possible, the chief manager should make this presentation—not only because he best knows the philosophies, and goals and objectives of the institution, but also because the new employee is psychologically impressed and more readily accepts such information when it comes from the chief administrator.

Specific Job Training

As soon as the new employee reports for work, the immediate supervisor begins training on the specific tasks of the job. Sometimes this training is given by the person leaving the job. This practice of having the former incumbent of the job train the new employee is risky, particularly if that departing employee has in any way been a problem. Having the departing employee do the training perpetuates his work habits and patterns. It also frequently establishes attitudes and opinions towards the supervisor, the department, and the organization. For these reasons it is recommended that the immediate supervisor accomplish the training of new employees.

There are many ways of training. The worst way is to describe verbally in a few minutes the tasks to be performed. The new employee, already flustered by being in a new environment with new responsibilities, probably will hear little of the supervisor's remarks. Some employees are able to observe other employees, to figure out the job from the job description, and to learn the job on their own in spite of the supervisor. Others fail, and such failure is the fault of the supervisor. If the employee has not learned, to paraphrase an old saying, the supervisor has not taught.

Any training given an employee must be carefully planned. The following six basic principles guide a good trainer:

1) The simple tasks must be taught first.
2) The task must be broken down into its basic components.
3) Only the correct procedures should be taught.

4) Teaching cycles should be short and should be reinforced by practice.
5) Skills should be developed through repetition.
6) The trainee should be motivated.

During World War II the War Manpower Commission developed a widely used system of job training called Job Instruction Training. While it sounds as if it is limited to routine or clerical tasks, the principles of JIT can be successfully applied to any form of training. The JIT consists of four basic steps, which are carried out by the trainer after careful preparation. This information is taken from the Commission's *Training within Industry Report.*[25]

First, here's what *you must* do to *get ready* to teach a job:
1. Decide what the learner must be taught in order to do the job efficiently, safely, economically and intelligently.
2. Have the right tools, equipment, supplies and material ready.
3. Have the work place properly arranged, just as the worker will be expected to keep it. Then you should *instruct* the learner by the following *four basic steps*:

STEP I–PREPARATION (of the learner)

1. Put the learner at *ease*.
2. Find out what he already knows about the job.
3. Get him interested and desirous of learning the job.

STEP II–PRESENTATION (of the operations and knowledge)

1. *Tell, Show, Illustrate*, and *Question* in order to put over the new knowledge and operations.
2. Instruct slowly, clearly, completely and patiently, one point at a time.
3. Check, question and repeat.
4. Make sure the learner really knows.

STEP III–PERFORMANCE TRY-OUT

1. Test learner by having him perform the job.
2. Ask questions beginning with *why, how, when* or *where*.
3. Observe performance, correct errors, and repeat instructions if necessary.
4. Continue until you *know he knows*.

STEP IV–FOLLOW-UP

1. Put him "on his own."
2. Check frequently to be sure he follows instructions.
3. Taper off extra supervision and close follow-up until he is qualified to work with normal supervision.

REMEMBER–If the learner hasn't learned, the teacher hasn't taught.

Continuing Institutional Training

Periodically, following the initial orientation meetings described above, the institution provides continuing training programs for new employees and for selected groups of employees. The new employees need more orientation to the institution than just the general orientation. They need to have an understanding of the responsibilities of the various organizational units of the library. Such units as the personnel office, the public information office, and the various subject or functional departments are described so that the employee sees their role in the total organization. These training sessions are usually conducted by the manager of the unit being discussed. The techniques of using visual presentations and of permitting extensive discussion and questioning will make such sessions productive.

On a recurring basis, as specific training needs are identified, selected groups of employees are called together. These groups frequently consist of department managers and sub-managers. Training might cover such topics as how to prepare performance evaluation reports, how to conduct good performance evaluation interviews, how to prepare departmental budget recommendations, or how to do task analysis for job description revision. These training sessions concerning all units of the organization may be conducted by a specialist from within the institution or by an authority brought into the institution for this specific program.

All of the training programs described above are developed and presented by the institution. Many training and educational programs outside the institution must be available to employees. Attendance at local, regional, and national conferences and workshops provides opportunities for employee development and growth. But at the present time, when the role and responsibility of libraries of all types is changing, more structured forms of training or educational experiences must be made available. Many institutions provide tuition funds for employees who take formal courses that are job related. The necessity for an employee to do study beyond the first professional degree is increasing constantly as library operations become more complex.

Every library, regardless of size or type, needs a planned, continuing training program. Such activities are not haphazardly scheduled but are organized on a structured continuum. Such programs provide the means by which employees can grow on the job and be ready to advance as local opportunities become available. Through such programs employers are able to identify employees who are potential supervisors and to prepare them for such responsibility.

FOOTNOTES

[1] Saul W. Gellerman, *The Management of Human Relations* (New York: Holt, Rinehart and Winston, 1966), p. 27.

[2] Ibid., p. 28.

[3] Ibid., p. 32.

[4] Ibid., p. 34.

[5] Rensis Likert, *New Patterns of Management* (New York: McGraw-Hill, 1966).

[6] Gellerman, *Management of Human Relations*, p. 39.

[7] Abraham H. Maslow, *Motivation and Personality*, 2nd ed. (New York: Harper and Row, 1970), pp. 35ff.

[8] Douglas McGregor, *The Human Side of Enterprise* (New York: McGraw-Hill, 1960), Chapters 3 and 4.

[9] Douglas McGregor, *Leadership and Motivation* (Cambridge, Mass.: M.I.T. Press, 1966), pp. 5-6.

[10] Ibid., p. 15.

[11] Edgar H. Schein, *Organizational Psychology* (Englewood Cliffs, N.J.: Prentice-Hall, 1965), pp. 49-63.

[12] Harold Koontz, and Cyril O'Donnell, *Principles of Management*, 4th ed. (New York: McGraw-Hill, 1968), pp. 544-545.

[13] Likert, *New Patterns*, Chapter 8.

[14] Ibid., p. 105.

[15] Saul W. Gellerman, *Management by Motivation* (Chicago: American Management Association, 1968).

[16] George S. Odiorne, *Personnel Administration by Objectives* (Homewood, Ill.: Richard D. Irwin, 1971).

[17] Frederick Herzberg, Bernard Mausner, and Barbara Bloch Snyderman, *The Motivation to Work* (New York: John Wiley, 1959), p. 60.

[18] L. F. Carter, "On Defining Leadership," in C. G. Browne and T. S. Cohn (eds.), *The Study of Leadership* (Danville, Ill.: Interstate Printers and Publishers, 1955).

[19] P. Selznick, *Leadership in Administration* (New York: Harper and Row, 1957), p. 63.

[20] Peter Drucker, *The Effective Executive* (New York: Harper and Row, 1967), Chapter 1.

[21] C. I. Bernard, *The Functions of the Executive* (Cambridge, Mass.: Harvard University Press, 1938).

[22] Claude E. Shannon, and Warren Weaver, *The Mathematical Theory of Communication* (Urbana: University of Illinois Press, 1949).

[23] William B. Wolf, *The Management of Personnel* (Belmont, Calif.: Wadsworth Publishing Co., 1961).

[24] Jurgen Ruesch, and Weldon Kees, *Non-Verbal Communication* (Berkeley: University of California Press, 1956), p. 189.

[25] War Manpower Commission, The Training within Industry Report (Washington, D.C.: Bureau of Training, Training within Industry Service, War Manpower Commission, 1945), p. 195.

6
PRINCIPLES OF CONTROL

Some distinction must be made first between control and controls. The two are very much interrelated, effective control within an organization being dependent upon the types of controls that have been established. Control as a function is greatly emphasized in many organizations and by some schools of thought. Organizations that emphasize control view the manager as being ultimately responsible for the results of the organization, therefore he has to control carefully everything and everyone within the organization. The synonym of control, then, is direction, while a definition of "controls" might be measurement to provide information. The former, according to Drucker, pertains to an end while the latter is the means; the first is concerned with events and the other with facts; one is analytical and operational, concerned with what was and is, while the other deals with expectations.[1]

The concept of control is most evident in all types of libraries through their overall governing authorities. In academic libraries this direction is exercised through such regulatory groups as trustees and the chancellor or president and, to a lesser extent, by the faculty (through a faculty library committee) and the students (through a student library committee). The library is legally bound by the constitutional provisions, charters, articles of incorporation, and general or special laws applicable to the institution as a whole. In special or industrial libraries this function is exercised through one of the divisions of the organization—usually the research division, the sales division, or the manufacturing division. The controlling body is the corporate or company board of directors. Public libraries and school libraries are controlled by their city manager or superintendent, and the city council or school committee. These are all controlling agents for the library because of their total institutional charge and because of their funding responsibilities. Internal control of the library organization rests with the management—both the administration and the line supervisors within the library. Besides those bodies directly related to the controlling function within the organization, numerous outside groups are involved in such aspects as standards, certification, and accreditation of libraries and librarians. For example, the higher education accrediting bodies such as the North Central Association of College and Secondary Schools have an influence on the libraries of institutions they accredit; the American Library Association has influence both through the establishment of standards for different types of libraries and library services and through its Committee on Accreditation, which is responsible for setting standards for library education; state departments of education establish guidelines for the certification of school librarians or media specialists; and specialized interest groups, such as the Medical Library Association, set certification standards for their members.

Other laws include local, state, and national ones that regulate such aspects as planning, constructing, and maintaining library buildings through municipal ordinances and regulations, building codes, zoning and fire regulations. Broader legislation includes, for instance, copyright and federal funding legislation, which places certain control on the operation of the library.

These groups exist primarily to regulate the activities of the library and to measure, to one extent or another, the actions and output of the organization.

Other bodies that exert some external control on libraries include unions and political bodies. Through collective bargaining, unions can regulate hiring, salaries, working conditions, fringe benefits, etc., and political bodies can influence the appointments of individuals or the disbursal of funds within the library. Extreme pressures are often placed on libraries by outside bodies, both in the hiring of new staff and in issues relating to collection development, censorship and intellectual freedom, and library services and facilities. The "Friends of the Library" group is a good example of an organization that may expect to have some say in the directions the library will take in return for their charitable contributions.

REQUIREMENTS FOR ADEQUATE CONTROL

Controls are concerned with locating operational weakness and taking corrective action. Control implies the existence of goals and plans; in fact, no organization can be effectively controlled without that element. The most effective control prevents deviations from those plans by anticipating that such deviations will occur unless immediate action is taken. Controls are important in any organization, but they are particularly important in a large organization to provide managers with facts in a comprehensible form and at the time when they are required. The term controls, unfortunately, is often interpreted as restrictions or restraints to be forced on the system; in the strictly theoretical sense, however, they are guides for the organization and they indicate how effectively the organization is progressing toward meeting its established goals.

Fayol's definition is still useful:

> The control of an undertaking consists of seeing that everything is being carried out in accordance with the plan which has been adopted, the orders which have been given, and the principles which have been laid down. Its object is to point out mistakes in order that they may be rectified and prevented from occurring again.[2]

To be effective, controls must be objective and must reflect the job they are to perform. The library should strive for control techniques that forecast deviations early enough so that corrections can be made before the problem occurs; at the least, the controls should point up exceptions at critical points. In addition, any controls system that does not pose corrective actions after deviations occur is little more than an interesting exercise. Controls, wherever they are found and whatever they control, involve three basic steps: establishing standards, measuring performance against standards, and correcting deviations.

Establishing Standards

Standards fall into two basic classes—those relating to material (including quality, quantity, cost, and time) and those relating to moral aspects (including ethical criteria that may be used to establish some sort of code of ethics). Standards are established criteria against which actual results can be measured. They may be physical and represent quantities of products, units of service, man-hours, etc., which can be evidenced through time and motion studies of library operations; they may be stated in monetary terms such as costs, revenues or investments, etc., which are evidenced through record keeping and budget preparation; or they may be expressed in any other terms that measure performance, such as performance rating systems. General standards, such as those proposed by the American Library Association, are important as guides but they do not provide meaningful evaluation for the individual library for a number of reasons. Hamburg's study points out this weakness:

1. Most of the standards are descriptive in nature . . .

2. Most of the standards that prescribe quantitative objectives are arbitrarily formulated . . .

3. The emphasis of the standards is directed toward evaluating the input resources of the library . . .

4. The standards discourage experimentation with different programs and different allocations of input resources . . . [3]

Some standards are nebulous and almost impossible to measure, such as the loyalty of an employee to the library's objectives. If the scientific method is to be used, then standards must be measurable. In any case, to be effective standards should be acceptable to those whose performance is being regulated. The process should be explained and agreed upon rather than forced. If standards are forced some resistance will surely occur.

Measurement of Performance against Standards

There are many activities for which it is extremely difficult to develop sound standards and there are many that are hard to measure. Others—for instance, the number of titles cataloged in a month, or the number of volumes circulated—are easy to measure. What is important here is to keep accurate records of what is done. If records are not kept, if the output cannot be measured objectively, then it is difficult to assess the amount that the actual performance deviates from the planned performance. This feedback is an important factor in the controlling process.

There are two basic types of control—preventative and feedback. "Preventative control processes, as the name implies, attempt to prevent deviations from developing in the conduct of organizational behavior. Feedback control processes rely on information from actual performance and are designed to correct deviations after they have developed."[4]

Figure 6-1
Simplified Feedback Process

A simplified example of detecting deviations in libraries might be a monthly budget balance sheet that shows that in the month of July three-fourths of the amount budgeted for telephone for the year has already been expended and that unless corrective action is taken the library will go over the budgeted amount in that category. A decision must then be made on how to correct this.

The study of cybernetics, which has become increasingly important in the control feedback process, is applicable to a library situation. Cybernetics is basically a self-regulating method by which messages that the system sends to itself indicate deviations from the desired course. This may be expressed in a very simplified diagram (Figure 6-2), which shows how the information flow makes possible the self-regulation of the system.

Figure 6-2
Communications Process in a Feedback System

Communication is the most important aspect because it involves transmitting and receiving messages or information—in this case, data used to make the decisions that control the system's behavior.

Correction of Deviation

Once standards have been agreed upon and some sort of analysis has been performed to measure the activity against the standard, the next step is to correct any deviations from that norm which might be occurring. This correction can be achieved by exercising organizational prerogative, for instance, in the case of personnel, by reassignment or clarification of duties, by additional staffing, by better selection and training of staff, or by some other method of restaffing.

TECHNIQUES OF CONTROL

When one thinks of internal controls, mechanical controls come to mind first, including circulation control, automated acquisitions, etc. These technological controls are only one example of tools that are being used to measure library operations. The computer has become an invaluable aid to decision making, particularly for larger library organizations. It has been used effectively, although in a limited number of situations, in establishing models for library operations through decision theory, game theory, graph theory, queueing theory, and simulation exercises. Many more basic techniques and tools are being employed in the control process in the library, particularly as libraries become more "accountable" for their operations. These include such varying operations as cost benefit analysis, operational research, and budgeting. Since some of these are rather sophisticated techniques, often applicable only to large library systems, they will be only briefly mentioned here.

Cost Benefit Analysis

The technique of cost benefit is simply one of choosing from alternatives when measurement in dollars or other specific measures may not be possible. Even in those cases, however, some measures can and should be established. For instance, if the objective is the improvement of referral service at the information desk, effectiveness can be measured by the number of personal and telephone inquiries answered or unanswered and the judgment of staff as to patrons' satisfaction with services offered. The emphasis of cost effectiveness is on output; each alternative is weighed in terms of effectiveness or costs against the objective that has been set. In some cases, cost models can be developed to show cost estimates for each alternative, or effectiveness models can be developed to show relationships between the alternatives and their effectiveness.

Time and Motion Study

Motion study enables a library system to record in flow chart form the present method of doing something, to analyze its effectiveness, and then from this analysis to improve the method. The new method can then be timed to report the performance standard. Time studies complement motion studies in determining performance standards. The third element in this quantifying process is that of cost—that is, attaching a dollar figure to the activities of an individual. Both time and cost vary with the level of the individual performing the task and the institution in which the work is taking place. Many time and motion studies have been done in libraries, particularly relating to routine tasks such as pasting pockets in books, typing subject headings on pre-printed cards, preparing items for the bindery, etc.

Operations Research

Operation research which grew out of the military needs of World War II, occupies the interest of a number of different groups, particularly statisticians and mathematicians.

> The operations researchers soon joined forces with the mathematical economists who had come into the same area—to the mutual benefit of both groups . . . No meaningful line can be drawn any more to demarcate operations research from scientific management or scientific management from management science.[5]

During the late 1960s and early 1970s, applied operational research has come into its own in the library decision-making process. This is primarily because in recent years decision making in general has emphasized the mathematical and statistical approach rather than an approach based on matter of judgment. This has been made possible primarily by technological development and the application of scientific methods. Conceptual "MODELS" for decision making are simply attempts to simulate reality. These are powerful means of testing various alternatives without changing the commitments involved in a typical decision. The primary approach of operations research consists of a broad view of the problem by the whole organization; this is succeeded by a team approach, using personnel with different backgrounds from different departments.

As this technique relates to control, its major contribution has been in constructing models that can be used in the decision-making process. To accomplish this, a basic knowledge of systems analysis is necessary. Again, the important first step, as in most techniques, is to identify objectives and then to look at variables that might influence the objectives. These are then expressed mathematically to determine the best alternative in terms of the objectives set. The current system in use is described. Based upon this analysis, a series of mathematical models are developed to describe the interrelationship within the organization. Data are then collected to measure the system or, if data are not available, assumptions or speculations are made. This information provides the basis for a working model for a new system. With this information in hand, the librarian is then able to make decisions based on the alternatives presented. The analytical statistical technique and the techniques of probability theory are employed.

As Chen points out, "the greatest potential of the techniques of operations research lies in predicting the future by employing the mathematical models developed rather than in knowing the present by analyzing the past experimental data."[6] Because of the technique's complexity and its use of mathematics and computers, most librarians have not yet reached the point of applying operations research to improve managerial control.

There are limits to this approach. The quantitative method can be no better than the assumptions and estimates used in reaching the solution. Also, this method demands some knowledge of mathematics and statistical concepts, and these are areas where librarians in general are at their weakest. We have relied heavily on non-librarians to provide this expertise. Finally, it should be remembered that use of quantitative tools concerns only one phase of the decision-making process. It is a kind of "management information" that is seldom used to identify the problem or develop alternatives.

One technique used by operations researchers is linear programming, though certain conditions must exist to make its use effective: "1) Goals must be stated in mathematical terms; 2) Alternatives must be available and stated; 3) Resources are usually limited; 4) Variables must be interrelated."[7] Sometimes the cost of such an approach outweighs the benefits, because it is often difficult if not impossible to quantify data. "Linear programming is concerned with optimizing a decision problem by analyzing interrelationships of system components and contributions of these components to the objective function."[8]

Other techniques are the Queueing Theory, or waiting-line theory (which could be applied in studying peak periods at circulation desks); the Monte Carlo technique, which is used to simulate an environment and then determine the results that certain decisions would provide within that environment; and the Decision Tree, which is part of the Decision Theory approach. Those interested in these and other techniques are encouraged to consult basic texts on those tools.

PERT

One other technique of control in the planning process, which is highly applicable to library operations, is that of PERT (Program Evaluation and Review Technique), developed by the U.S. Navy's Special Projects Office to plan the Polaris Weapon System. This technique consists of enumerating events whose completion can be measured. "Most likely" times are then calculated for the accomplishment of each event, so that one can see how long it would take for the progression of events to be completed. This model-building network approach is most effectively used for major projects that are one-time *events*. An example would be the opening of a new branch library. Activities can be plotted to allow the librarian to determine the most expeditious route—or critical path—that can be taken to finish the event. Just as with other techniques already discussed, in PERT one must be able to state objectives, then activities must be enumerated and estimates must be given for the time required for each of these *activities*. An abbreviated two-path diagram serves to illustrate the concept (Figure 6-3).

Figure 6-3
Simplified Two-Path PERT Diagram

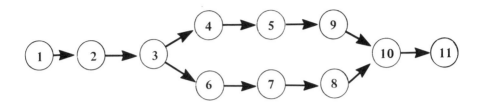

This would suggest that there are two paths to be taken—say, from the time the idea of a branch library is formulated until the building is ready for occupancy (◯ represents events and ⟶ represents activities). Times would be assigned for each activity (say, three weeks between events 4 and 5, while time between 6 and 7 may be one week). This suggests to the librarian that either path 1, 2, 3, 4, 5, 9, 10, 11 or path 1, 2, 3, 6, 7, 8, 10, 11 can be taken. If time is of the essence, the shorter route might be more desirable. At any rate, this technique allows one to analyze a project in depth before it is initiated. This not only gives the decision maker an idea of the time frame involved but also aids in identifying potential weaknesses.

The biggest disadvantage of PERT is its overemphasis on time and almost complete lack of attention to cost. This disadvantage has led to the development of PERT/COST, which introduces the *cost* factor into the process. When the system to be studied is complex and when a number of events are involved, it becomes very expensive to establish a cost for each event. PERT is used mainly in industry, but some library systems have begun to explore its value in their planning process, particularly if that operation is a complex and lengthy one.

This brief discussion in no way presents the importance or potential for these controls, and does not even begin to present all of the variations that those systems have produced. However, since volumes have been written on each of the topics, it would be almost impossible to cover their potential adequately in this volume. Readers interested in these subjects should consult those headings in the library literature for a fuller discussion. As mentioned earlier in this chapter, the computer is having great influence on the management of library operation. The effects of electronic data processing on circulation control, acquisitions of library materials, serials control, etc., are significant. In addition, computerized services such as the on-line cataloging through OCLC, BALLOTS, and others, and access to bibliographic data bases enable libraries to measure more adequately service output and costs.

BUDGETARY CONTROL

The budget is perhaps the best and most important control device in existence to measure programs and their effectiveness within the library. Funds for the organization's operation, depending on the type of library or information system, come from local, state, regional, or national sources, from foundation support or endowments, from tuition or gifts, or from a number of other sources. These funds may come to the library directly or to the parent organization, which then designates them for library use. Determination of that amount is usually based on expressed needs, which are justified by services offered or projected or, to a lesser extent, on standards that have been established for particular types of libraries—particularly ALA standards for public, school, junior college and college libraries.

One good definition of budgetary control is that used by the International Management Institute, which defines it as a method of rationalization whereby estimates covering different periods of time are, by the study of statistical records and analytical research of all kinds, established for all and everything that affects the life of a business concern and that can be expressed in figures.

Budgeting in libraries, which is usually on a yearly cycle, is the primary means by which formulated plans can be carried out. Many types of budgets are not really applicable to libraries, since libraries are not primarily profit-making institutions. However, several different types of approaches to budgeting are being used in libraries, and these will be discussed.

One great danger in budgeting is the problem of disguised needs. Libraries often are accused of asking for much more than they actually need; indeed, they often do tend to base current budget justifications on past budgets. In other words, if a library spent a certain amount last year for equipment, that amount becomes this year's floor from which to work, even though the same kind and extent of equipment may not be needed this year. This kind of thinking often leads to automatic reductions in library budgets by those who hold the purse strings, whether they are city managers, college presidents, or school superintendents.

The budgeting process is often a time-delay process and is usually prepared one year—or in some cases two or three years—in advance. In those instances, it is extremely difficult to project what the needs will be three years from now, even if one has done some long-range planning. In most cases, a library must follow the budget system and budgeting cycle that has been adapted by the larger system, whether that is the university, college, city government, school district, or corporation.

The types of budgets discussed here are presented as unique; most often, however, a combination of budgeting systems is used. Although many libraries now have a separate staff concerned primarily with budgets and the accounting process, most libraries involve a number of employees in the budget-planning process. Budget requests for programs or units are frequently estimated by the supervisors most familiar with that aspect of the operation. A coordinating agent—either the director, his representative, or a committee—is responsible for pulling these budget requests into a total budget and presenting it to the funding authority so that they can understand and, it is hoped, support the budget. Timetables for budget preparation and presentation are essential so that wide impact can be gained.

The budgetary aspect of control becomes even more important as costs rise. With rising costs, librarians are forced to prepare comprehensive reports on the financial status so that effective allocation can be made and accurate projections can be made for future funding.

Libraries are finding themselves forced to seek alternative routes for funding. These include federal and state funding, as well as private foundation and individual citizen funding. A new political role, with extensive public relations requirements, is being forced on libraries.

BUDGETING TECHNIQUES FOR LIBRARIES

Library budgeting techniques fall into several groups. These include both the traditional approaches used by many organizations and the more innovative techniques that have only recently found their ways into libraries. As these newer techniques are considered, it must be kept in mind that it is always costly to switch from one system to another. Therefore, the advantages of a different system must be clear before one decides to switch from the old system.

Line-Item

Probably the most common type of budget is that approach which divides expenditures into broad categories, such as salaries and wages, materials and supplies, equipment, capital expenditures, and miscellaneous, with further sub-divisions within these categories. It is possible to designate items within these categories to such a degree that it becomes difficult, if not impossible, to shift them; thus, this system can be inflexible to innovation. For example, within the broad category of "materials and supplies" it may become desirable to add subscription money for new periodicals after the budget has been set. One might wish to accomplish this by transferring money from equipment, since it has now been determined that one can do without an additional typewriter. This kind of transfer is usually frowned upon by budgeting authorities, however; if it is not completely discouraged, it is often made very difficult to accomplish because of the paper work and red tape involved.

There are several advantages to the line-item approach. For one thing, line-item budgets are easy to prepare. Most are done by projecting current expenditures to next year, taking cost increases into account. This type of budget is also easy to understand and to justify, since it can be shown that the allocated funds were spent in the areas for which they were budgeted. A request to open a new position or to increase the supplies budget by 10 percent because that is the average amount that postage, telephone charges, etc., went up last year, can be understood by the funding authority. The greatest disadvantage to the line-item approach is that there is almost no relationship at all between the request and the objectives of the organization. Using the line-item approach simply projects the past and present into the future. An example of a line-item budget is given in Figure 6-4.

Figure 6-4
Line-Item Budget Summary Sheet

BUDGET REQUEST FORM 1

SUMMARY

Department or Program: Library

Department No.: 02876

For Fiscal Year: 1976-77

Control No.	Expenditures	Actual Prior Year 1974-75	Budget Current Year 1975-76	Budget Request Next Year 1976-77	Budget Approved Next Year 1976-77
100	Salaries	138,000	139,000	150,000	
102	Wages	11,000	11,500	12,000	
103	Staff benefits	20,700	20,850	22,500	
108	Contracted Services	3,500	3,500	4,000	
109	Telephone Services	5,700	5,800	6,000	
111	Office Equipment	1,000	1,300	1,200	
112	Office Supplies	7,800	8,000	8,500	
113	Travel	2,800	2,800	3,000	
114	Instructional Supplies	90,000	93,000	96,000	
	TOTAL	280,500	$285,750	$303,200	

Lump Sum

A commonly used variation on the traditional approach is the lump sum approach. In this form of budgeting, a certain dollar amount is allocated to the library, and it becomes the responsibility of the library to decide how that sum is broken into categories that can be identified. These categories are usually the same ones mentioned under line-item budgeting: salaries and wages, materials and supplies, equipment, capital expenditures, and miscellaneous or overhead. This might seem more flexible than line-item budgeting, but it still does not relate the objectives to services. Libraries using this technique are forced to develop programs within the dollar figure allocated, instead of the other way around.

Formula Budgets

Formula budgeting uses some predetermined standards for allocation of monetary resources. Such an approach has been adopted by several large library systems with the thought that once the criteria have been established they can be applied across the board to all units within the library system. Allen surmises that the reason for the popularity of formula—over PPBS—is:

1. Formula is mechanical and easy to prepare.
2. Because of its application to all institutions in the political jurisdiction, there appears to be justification for monies requested.
3. The governing bodies have a sense of equity because each institution in the system is measured against the same criteria.
4. Fewer budgeting and planning skills are required to prepare and administer a formula budget.[9]

These formulae, which are usually expressed in terms of a percentage of the total institutional cost, focus on input rather than activities. For instance, the budget-related standard of the Standards for College Libraries states that "experience has shown that library budgets, exclusive of capital costs and the costs of physical maintenance, which fall below six percent of the college's total educational and general expenditures, are seldom able to sustain the range of library programs required by the institution."[10] Other formulae have applied a fixed dollar figure per full-time equivalent student and faculty, or have attached collection and staff figures to programs offered.

Formula budgeting in libraries probably had its impetus with the Clapp-Jordan formula,[11] which developed a theoretical model for measuring the adequacy of library resources. Other formulae have developed since then—most notably the Michigan system formula,[12] the California University formula[13] and the Washington State formula.[14] Perhaps the most recent one is that developed by the Standards for College Libraries,[15] which relates to holdings (Formula A), Staff (Formula B), and Facilities (Formula C). The formulae that have developed vary in their degrees of sophistication. Some functions cannot be related to to those formulae and must receive separate justification. Perhaps the biggest fallacy in such an approach is that it assumes a relationship between the quantity being expressed and the quality of service. Several state systems now use or contemplate using some type of formula budget.

Program Budgeting

A relatively new concept in budgeting for libraries is the idea of program budgeting, which is concerned with the organization's activites, not with individual items or expenditures, which were the concern of the approaches discussed above. Such a budget is presented so that the library's activities are emphasized, and dollars can then be assigned to programs or services provided. For example, if a public library system provides bookmobile service for the community, the cost of that service (staffing, materials, overhead, etc.) is calculated. In this way one can see just what the bookmobile service is costing. Based on the total program, one can decide whether to continue, modify, or delete the service. An example of a Program Budget is given in Figure 6-5.

Performance Budgeting

A technique similar to program budgeting is that of performance budgeting, which bases expenditures on the performance of activities and emphasizes efficiency of operations. This approach requires the careful accumulation of quantitative data, over a period of time. Techniques of cost benefit analysis are required to measure the performance and establish norms. Performance budgeting has been criticized because in it the economy aspect overshadows the service aspect. This approach is sometimes called function budgeting, because costs are presented in terms of work to be accomplished. A good example of this would be processing materials—from submission of an order until the time that the volume is on the shelf and the cards are in the catalog. All activities involved (verifying the author, title, etc.; ordering, receiving, cataloging and classifying, providing book pockets, call number and catalog cards; filing cards in catalog and placing volume on shelf) can be analyzed as to average time for the activity and average cost per item. Therefore, careful cost and work measurements can be applied to each activity. Fixed costs of building maintenance, heating, lights, equipment used, etc.—which are variable but are directly related to the work being done—must also be added to the final cost. This approach measures quantity rather than quality of service.

Planning Programming Budgeting System (PPBS)

PPBS is a technique that was originally developed by Rand Corporation and was introduced into the Department of Defense by Robert McNamara in 1961. President Johnson directed all principal government agencies to implement it, and by 1965 it was being used by all of these agencies. Many complex organizations, of which libraries are a part, are now using PPBS or some modified form of it. These include state and local governments, college and university systems, and industry.

PPBS is a technique that combines the best of both program budgeting and performance budgeting. The emphasis in this approach is on planning. It begins with the establishment of goals and objectives, just as in program budgeting, but the controlling aspect of measurement, which is paramount in performance budgeting,

Figure 6-5
Program Budget Sheet

Page from Program Budget

Organization: County Library

Program: Bookmobile Service

Objective: This service is offered to county residents who reside more than three miles from a public library. Specific services offered include providing basic reference collection of encyclopedias, dictionaries and handbooks and a rotating collection of circulating materials on a variety of subjects for all levels of readers. Makes two stops per day, covers seven miles, five days per week.

Personnel Service

Librarian	$11,000
Driver	7,500
Stock boy (to load, unload truck, 4 hrs. per week @ $2.50 x 52 weeks)	520
Benefits	2,775
SUB-TOTAL	$21,795

Materials

Books (2,000 collection x $10 average + $4.50 processing costs)	29,000
Periodicals (10 subscriptions @ $10 each)	100
SUB-TOTAL	$29,100

Other

Vehicle depreciation	1,000
Maintenances, gasoline (30 mi. per week x 52 weeks x 15¢ per mile) oil, insurance, etc.	571
TOTAL	$52,466

is also part of PPBS. It emphasizes the cost of accomplishing goals (programs) set by the library instead of stressing objects, which the more traditional budgets highlight. This approach forces one to think of the budget as a tool to allocate resources rather than to control operations.

The steps important in PPBS are:

1. Identifying the objectives of the library.
2. Presenting alternative ways to achieve those objectives—with cost benefit ratios presented for each.
3. Identifying the activities that are necessary for each program.
4. Evaluating the result so that corrective actions can be taken.

This is a reemphasis of the desired steps in the control process already discussed. An example might be given of a particular library's preliminary development of a PPBS approach (see Figure 6-6).

Figure 6-6
Library Service Measurement Framework (LSMF)*

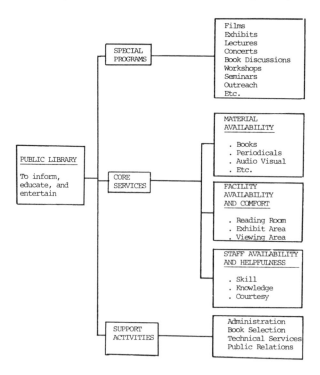

(Model developed by Dr. Robert DeNoble on the basis of work done at Peat, Marwick, Mitchell & Co., Boston)

*Reproduced with permission.

In essence, this scientific approach to budgeting improves the decision-making process, which calls for systematic analysis of alternative ways of meeting objectives. The crux of the PPB system is the selection of appropriate criteria for evaluating each alternative against relevant objectives; it combines the functions of planning (identifying objectives), translating that to a program (staff and materials), and finally, stating those requirements in budgetary terms (financing). Headings for a PPBS Summary Sheet are shown in Figure 6-7.

Figure 6-7
PPBS Summary Sheet Headings

County of:	PROGRAM SUMMARY
Operating Budget: (Year)	
Program: (Title of Program)	
Goal: (Brief operational goal)	
Description: (Brief description of Program)	

Such an approach allows the librarian to enumerate programs and assign costs to those programs. It also allows funding agencies to place programs into perspective and to evaluate the effects of cutting monies from or adding monies to the budget.

A good example of a modified PPBS approach is the Vigo County Public Library (Indiana) summary of activities, which indicates eight program categories (see Figure 6-8).

ACCOUNTING AND REPORTING

The final aspect of budgeting is that of keeping accurate records of what has been disbursed, what has been encumbered, and what remains. This is usually achieved through monthly records prepared by the accounting office—either as a part of the library or as a part of the larger organization, such as the city government. These monthly statements can act as benchmarks to tell the library staff how they are progressing towards the objectives, if they have been stated, or simply to tell the library staff how much remains of the budget figure.

This monthly summary statement, or balance sheet, is the procedure used in most organizations. Along with accounting goes the important element of reporting—reporting to the funding authority, reporting to the staff, and reporting

Figure 6-8
Community Use of a Public Library*

Community Use of the Vigo County Public Library for the Six Months' Period January to June 1969

Input Cost	Service Category	Program Objective	Output Totals	Cost per Output
$92,866	SELF SERVICE	Provide facilities, library materials and equipment.	203,587 persons	$ .45
$77,524	LENDING SERVICE	Lend library materials for home and office use.	324,481 items	$ .24
$42,398	INDIVIDUAL SERVICE	Furnish information, reader advisory, and reference assistance.	40,301 persons	$ 1.05
$ 7,878	ALERTING SERVICE	Promote awareness of the library and use of its resources.	908 productions	$ 8.67
$ 5,202	OUTREACH SERVICE	Provide library materials for the physically or environmentally handicapped.	10 stations	$520.20
$14,288	CONTROL SERVICE	Maintain control of materials through registration of patrons and overdue reminders to borrowers.	12,173 persons	$ 1.17
$20,106	GROUP SERVICE	Provide specialized services to groups, agencies, and organizations.	459 groups	$ 43.80
$ 3,720	RESEARCH SERVICE	Perform research service for public officials, ministers, business and industry managers, labor and other civic leaders.	150 researchers	$ 24.80

*Reprinted by permission of the American Library Association from "Toward PPBS in the Public Library," Edward N. Howard, *American Libraries*, April 1971, p. 391, copyrighted © 1971 by the American Library Association.

to the community. These reporting procedures can take a variety of forms—formal written reports with detailed statistical documentation, or informal reports (through memos, staff meetings, newspaper articles, etc.). It is at this point that the librarian's public relations responsibility becomes most evident. Only through a conscientious, positive approach of selling the library and its services can the librarian hope to maintain a level of activity and funding; and it is to be hoped that the approach can be so convincing that the support for those activities will even be increased. Public relations for librarians, then, is an art through which information and persuasion solicit public support for the causes that have been set forth in the goals of the library. Public relations is an integral part of the goals and objectives and the budgeting procedures in a library. More specifically, the publicity aspect (to staff, students, faculty, the public at large, and particularly benefactors) must be attractive and to the point. This is the library's primary means of gaining and holding the support necessary to develop programs.

FOOTNOTES

[1] Peter F. Drucker, "Controls, Control and Management," in C.P. Bonini, R.K. Jaedicke, and H.M. Wanger (eds.), *Managerial Controls: New Directions in Basic Research* (New York: McGraw-Hill, 1964), p. 286.

[2] Henri Fayol, *Industrial and General Administration* (Geneva: International Management Institute, 1929), p. 77.

[3] Morris Hamburg, *et al., Library Planning and Decision-Making Systems* (Philadelphia: University of Pennsylvania, 1974), pp. 38-39.

[4] W. Jack Duncan, *Essentials of Management* (Hinsdale, Ill.: Dryden Press, 1975), p. 408.

[5] Herbert A. Simon, *The New Science of Management Decision* (New York: Harper and Row, 1960), p. 15.

[6] Ching-Chih Chen, *Applications of Operations Research Models to Libraries* (Cambridge, Mass.: MIT Press, 1976), p. 3.

[7] Richard I. Levin, and Charles A. Kirkpatrick, *Quantitative Approaches to Management*, 2nd ed. (New York: McGraw-Hill, 1971), p. 161.

[8] Sang M. Lee, and L.J. Moore, *Introduction to Decision Science* (New York: Petrocelli-Charter, 1975), p. 90.

[9] Kenneth S. Allen, *Current and Emerging Budgeting Techniques in Academic Libraries* (Washington, D.C.: U.S. Department of Health, Education and Welfare, Office of Education, 1972), ED 071-726, p. 18.

[10] "Standards for College Libraries," in *College and Research Library News* 9 (October 1975): 298.

[11] Verner W. Clapp, and Robert J. Jordan, "Quantitative Criteria for Adequacy of Academic Library Collections," *College and Research Libraries* 26 (September 1965): 371-80.

[12] Robert E. Burton, "Formula Budgeting: An Example," *Special Libraries* 66 (February 1975): 61-67.

[13] University of California, Office of the Vice President for Finance, *Library Workload Measures* (Berkeley, Calif.: University of California, 1963), pp. 1-20. mimeo.

[14] University of Washington, Office of Interinstitutional Business Studies, *Model Budget Analysis System for Program 05 Libraries* (Olympia: University of Washington, 1970), pp. 1-16. mimeo.

[15] "Standards for College Libraries," pp. 277-79, 290-301.

[16] Edward N. Howard, "Toward PPBS in the Public Library," *American Libraries* 2, no. 4 (April 1971): 391.

7
LIBRARY MANAGEMENT DEVELOPMENT

Library management, as might be expected, shows no identifiable characteristic that would serve to set it apart from other organizational management. Trends, theories, and techniques introduced in management literature have slowly found their way into libraries. This development can be traced through a brief look at library literature.

In 1887 F.M. Cruden, then Librarian of the St. Louis Public Library, stated that "the duties of a chief executive of a library differ in no essential way from those of a manager of a stock company . . . the librarian may profit by the methods of the businessman."[1] Arthur E. Bostwick, addressing the New Zealand Library Association in 1911, advocated adoption of the methods of business efficiency in the operation of the library.[2] A number of other librarians, including Charles C. Williamson, emphasized the value to libraries of industrial methods, pointing out that "no one has attempted yet to treat comprehensively the principles and philosophy of library service or library management."[3] This was the period of development of the scientific management school, whose theories were applied to a number of industrial situations but not yet to libraries. It was not until the 1930s that particular attention was paid to the application of scientific management to libraries. Donald Coney emphasized the "new" approach by stating that " . . . scientific management furnishes library administrators with a useful instrument for orientating their activities."[4] Twenty years later, in 1954, Laurence J. Kipp published an article[5] that discussed the application of scientific management to library operations for the period of 1920 to 1950. Kittle, in his dissertation, points out that scientific management did not receive serious attention in libraries until after World War II.[6]

Ralph R. Shaw began his leading studies of the scientific management of library operations in the late 1940s and early 1950s. In one study he analyzed two trends in library management—specialization and integration of specialties into a functional organization.[7] These two conflicting trends, which he termed micromanagement and macromanagement, are still evident in library organization today. In 1954 Shaw, writing as editor of an issue of *Library Trends*, noted "a trend toward the application of scientific management techniques to public and research libraries, on time-and-motion studies, on standardization, and on management surveys."[8] Dougherty and Heinritz, students of Shaw, published the first full treatise on the application of scientific management to libraries.[9]

The influence of the human relations school became evident: the problems of people became as important as the mechanical procedures, and preparation for library administrators took on the personnel relations approach. An article by Danton[10] emphasized the trend toward analyzing the human side, where "personnel administration" became paramount to the democratization of the library organization. This was further expounded in a 1939 volume[11] on personnel administration. Among the recommendations were: greater attention to personnel administration; greater consideration of basic organization directed towards the simplification and coordination of activities; greater staff development; and better working conditions.[12]

The McDiarmids, in their writings of the late 1930s,[13] recognized two paramount problems in libraries—the need to delegate authority to the level of responsibility, and the need to define library objectives and their influence on the administration. Amy Winslow, in her 1953 paper, emphasized staff participation in "democratic organization."[14] Reese's article, directed to library administration, notes among other things an increase in staff participation in management of libraries.[15]

With respect to the social systems school, several works cited the development of library management in relation to the larger institution and the community the library serves. Joeckel, a pioneer in the field of library management, suggested that "library administrators will do well to seek models from comparative study in the fields of public administration, in business, in industry, and in education."[16] The Library Institute at which Joeckel's paper was presented was, perhaps, the landmark event in the analysis of library administration. Twenty years later, Wasserman supports Joeckel's contention that "... in a very real sense library administration is only an extension of public administration."[17]

Stone's survey has shown a tendency toward "emphasis upon theory and principles and basic functions, bringing with it corresponding de-emphasis upon specific technical skills."[18] This is substantiated when one examines the volumes that have been published in the last several years on organization and administration of specific types of libraries—academic, public, school, and special. In this regard, the Association of Research Libraries, through funding from the Council on Library Resources, has developed its Office of Management Studies, which is responsible for a number of projects relating to library management. One primary activity has been the issuing of "SPEC KITS" (currently over 20) on such topics as goals and objectives, collective bargaining, acquisition policies, etc. That office has also developed the self-study guide called "Management Review and Analysis," which was designed primarily to apply established management principles to libraries.

Finally, one must look at the quantitative or mathematical school and the influence it has had on library operations. During the late 1960s and into the 1970s managers of libraries have finally used applied operational research in their decision-making responsibilities.[19] It is evident that quantitative measures are having an impact on library management. Two recent reports illustrate this trend. In 1972 the Wharton School at the University of Pennsylvania finished a report which had been supported by a federal grant to design and develop a model for management information systems for universities and large public libraries.[20] That report classified library functions into seventeen categories, and it proposed that those categories be used as a basis for program budgeting systems in libraries. More recently Chen, in her dissertation, has demonstrated how operations research techniques can be used by library administrators in their everyday decision-making process.[21]

Recent issues of major research journals in librarianship make it clear that management "topics" are receiving increasing attention. A 1971 issue of *Library Trends* addresses itself to the dilemma of "How we can optimally integrate the technical and human resources that we manage toward achieving the library's service mission and, at the same time, manage working arrangements and role relationships so that people's needs for self-worth, growth, and development are significantly met in our libraries."[22] On that same topic, Stone researched a commissioned study for NCLIS.[23] An example, drawn from a number of volumes on the subject of personnel in libraries, is a report done for the Illinois State Library, which identifies the kinds of activities that are typical of the training and background of individuals working in libraries.[24]

Other special issues of *Library Trends* have been on "Effective Resource Allocation in Library Management,"[25] which addresses the issue of accountability in libraries; "Evaluation of Library Services," which examines "evaluative techniques and procedures used by librarians to determine the effectiveness of their programs (e.g., surveys, cost accounting, systems analysis, operations research, PPBS, MBO, PERT)";[26] and "Systems Design and Analysis for Libraries," which views systems analysis as a management tool to be used in "seeking out the fundamentals of a situation and applying to this study rigorous scientific methods, with the aim of finding an optimal solution to the problems facing managers."[27]

Finally, two works on networking give us the state of the art: one, "Resources and Bibliographic Support for a Nationwide Library Program,"[28] was commissioned by NCLIS; the other, now somewhat dated, is "Library Networks: Promise and Performance,"[29] which emphasizes the need for developing networks that include all types of libraries.

Perhaps the unit that is contributing the most, on a continuing basis, to the study of library management is the Association of Research Libraries. Through its University Library Management Studies Office it publishes "Occasional Papers" on relevant topics, and through its Management Studies Office it publishes SPEC (Systems and Procedures Exchange Center) flyers which have already been mentioned.

It is evident that the theories developed by the different schools (scientific management; human relations; quantitative) are being applied to library operations today. The continued use, development, and refinement of those thoughts and techniques will result in more efficient and effective library service.

FOOTNOTES

[1] Gertrude G. Drury, *The Library and Its Organization* (New York: H.W. Wilson Co., 1924), pp. 83-84.

[2] Arthur E. Bostwick, "Two Tendencies of American Library Work," *Library Journal* 36 (1911): 275-78.

[3] Charles C. Williamson, "Efficiency in Library Management," *Library Journal* 44 (1919): 76.

[4] Donald Coney, "Scientific Management in University Libraries," in G.T. Schwennig, ed., *Management Problems* (Chapel Hill, N.C.: University of North Carolina Press, 1930), p. 173.

[5] Lawrence J. Kipp, "Scientific Management in Research Libraries," *Library Trends* 2 (January 1954): 390-400.

[6] Arthur T. Kittle, "Management Theories in Public Administration in the United States," Ph.D. dissertation, Columbia University, 1961. [7]

[7] Ralph R. Shaw, "Scientific Management in the Library," *Wilson Library Bulletin* 21 (January 1947): 349-52.

[8] Ralph R. Shaw, "Scientific Management," *Library Trends* 2 (January 1954): 359-483.

[9] Richard M. Dougherty, and Fred J. Heinritz, *Scientific Management of Library Operations* (Metuchen, N.J.: Scarecrow Press, 1966).

[10] J. Periam Danton, "Our Libraries—The Trend Towards Democracy," *Library Quarterly* 4 (January 1934): 16-27.

[11] Clara W. Herbert, *Personnel Administration in Public Libraries* (Chicago: American Library Association, 1939).

[12] Ibid., pp. xiii-xiv.

[13] E.W. McDiarmid, and John M. McDiarmid, *The Administration of the American Public Library* (Chicago: American Library Association, 1943).

[14] Amy Winslow, "Staff Participation in Management," *Wilson Library Bulletin* 27 (April 1953): 624-28.

[15] Ernest J. Reese, ed. "Current Trends in Library Administration," *Library Trends* 7 (January 1959).

[16] C.B. Joeckel, ed. *Current Issues in Library Administration: Papers Presented Before the Library Institute at the University of Chicago*, August 1-12, 1938 (Chicago: University of Chicago Press, 1939), pp. vii-ix.

[17] Paul Wasserman, "Development of Administration in Library Service: Current Status and Future Prospects," *College and Research Libraries* 19 (November 1958): 288.

[18] Elizabeth W. Stone, *Training for the Improvement of Library Administration* (Urbana, Ill.: University of Illinois, Graduate School of Library Science, 1967), p. 15.

[19] Don R. Swanson, and Abraham Bookstein, eds., *Operations Research: Implications for Libraries* (Chicago: University of Chicago Press, 1972).

[20] Morris Hamburg, *et al.*, "Library Planning and Decision Making Systems," USOE Final Report, Project no. 8-0802 (Philadelphia: Wharton School, University of Pennsylvania, 1972). Monograph published by MIT Press.

[21] Ching-chih Chen, *Applications of Operations Research Models to Libraries* (Cambridge, Mass.: MIT Press, 1976).

[22] Elizabeth W. Stone, ed. "Personnel Development and Continuing Education in Libraries," *Library Trends* 20, no. 1 (July 1971): 3.

[23] U.S. National Commission on Libraries and Information Science, *Continuing Library and Information Science Education*, submitted by E. Stone *et al.* (Washington: ASIS, 1974).

[24] Myrl Ricking, and Robert E. Booth, *Personnel Utilization in Libraries: A Systems Approach* (Chicago: American Library Association, 1974).

[25] H. William Axford, "Effective Resource Allocation in Library Management," *Library Trends* 25, no. 4 (April 1975): 547-72.

[26] Sarah R. Reed, "Evaluation of Library Services," *Library Trends* 22, no. 3 (January 1974): 255.

[27] F. Wilfrid Lancaster, "Systems Design and Analysis for Libraries," *Library Trends* 21, no. 4 (April 1973): 463.

[28] U.S. National Commission on Libraries and Information Science, *Resources and Bibliographic Support for a Nationwide Library Program*, submitted by Vernon E. Palmour *et al.* (Rockville, Md.: Westat, Inc., 1974).

[29] Leon Carnovsky, ed., "Library Networks: Promise and Performance," *Library Quarterly* 39, no. 1 (January 1969): 1-108.